GOLF RESORTS

TOP OF THE WORLD VOLUME 2

edited by Martin Nicholas Kunz

with texts by Stefan Maiwald

teNeues

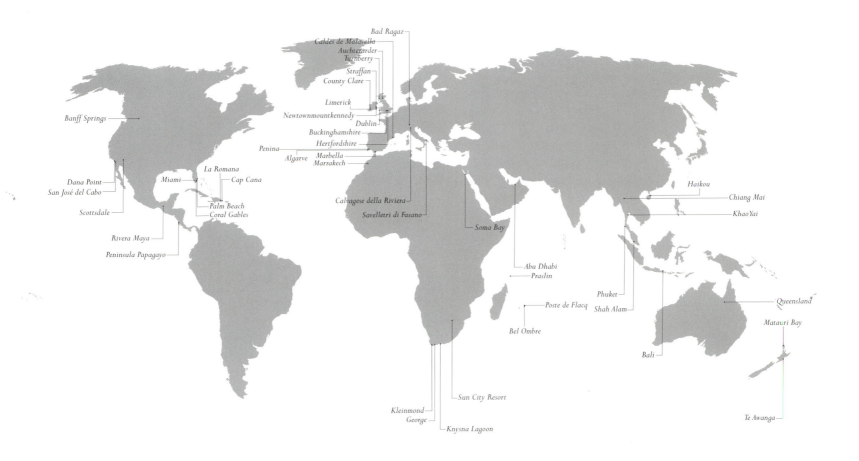

Banff Springs

Dana Point
San José del Cabo

Scottsdale

Miami

La Romana

Cap Cana

Palm Beach
Coral Gables

Rivera Maya

Peninsula Papagayo

Penina
Algarve
Marbella
Marrakech

Caldes de Malavella
Auchterarder
Turnberry
Straffan
County Clare
Limerick
Newtownmountkennedy
Dublin
Buckinghamshire
Hertfordshire

Bad Ragaz

Calvagese della Riviera
Savelletri di Fasano

Soma Bay

Abu Dhabi
Praslin

Poste de Flacq
Bel Ombre

Kleinmond
George
Knysna Lagoon

Sun City Resort

Haikou
Chiang Mai
KhaoYai

Phuket
Shah Alam

Bali

Queensland

Matauri Bay

Te Awanga

Golf Resorts

TOP OF THE WORLD VOLUME 2

Introduction

Golfers are people who embrace every aspect of life. They want to savor their vacation with all of their senses—intensely, exquisitely, and in all its colors. A golf vacation not only requires an excellent course, but also a place to enjoy the perfect drink after the game. A view of the sunset. Dinner under the stars. And the eagerness to discover what the next day might bring. The best golf resorts in the world guarantee outstanding play on perfectly maintained courses boasting an exciting design, but that is far from all: The service offered by the hotels introduced here meets the expectations of even the most discriminating guests and leaves nothing to be desired. Renowned chefs create Michelin-level cuisine; tired muscles are soothed in extravagant spas with cutting-edge treatments and millennium-old traditions. Guests not only find themselves rejuvenated for the next day, they also take away something very special that lasts far beyond their stay.

It comes as no surprise that golf travelers value the golf aspects of their vacation above all else. The resorts in this book are on the leading-edge in this respect as well: Former champions such as Jack Nicklaus, Gary Player, and Ray Floyd are the names behind many of the courses, while design stars such as Pete Dye and Tom Doak have created masterpieces out of fairways, bunkers, and greens in fairytale settings. Some resort golf courses, such as Turnberry in Scotland, Teeth of the Dog at Casa de Campo in the Dominican Republic, and Cape Kidnappers in New Zealand, are among the most beautiful courses in the world and regularly top the international "best of" lists. Other courses, such as the K Club, have written sport history, while Stoke Park provided the setting for what was perhaps the most famous match play in movie history when Sean Connery as James Bond faced off against Gert Fröbe as Auric Goldfinger.

Yet it is only when the frame is right that an artwork can truly shine. And only when all the elements work together seamlessly does a trip become an unforgettable experience. The golf resorts introduced here are sure to be remembered for a very long time because they are located amid the most spectacular scenery—from tropical dry forests to high deserts, from the Alps to the Mediterranean, and from the Indian Ocean to the Caribbean. After a round of golf, players can explore canyons, enjoy horseback rides along old Indian trails, conquer rough terrain on bicycle or in an off-road vehicle, dive down to coral reefs, admire the rainforest up close, sail along the coastline in a catamaran, or go on safari. For those who prefer a slower pace, the resorts offer myriad amenities that include private beach clubs, cozy rooms with fireplaces, libraries, and cigar lounges.

Unadulterated pleasure that extends far beyond the golf course: That is the promise made and gloriously kept by these resorts. Let the games begin!

Stefan Maiwald

Einleitung

Golfer sind Genussmenschen. Sie wollen ihren Urlaub mit allen Sinnen auskosten – intensiv, prachtvoll und farbenfroh. Zu einer Golfreise gehört vor allem ein guter Golfplatz, aber eben auch der perfekte Drink im Anschluss an die Runde. Der Blick auf die untergehende Sonne. Das Dinner unter dem Sternenhimmel. Und die Gespanntheit darauf, was der nächste Tag wohl bringen möge. Die besten Golf-Resorts der Welt garantieren großartigen Sport auf perfekt gepflegten, spannend gestalteten Kursen, doch das ist noch längst nicht alles: Der Service in den vorgestellten Hotels genügt den verwöhntesten Ansprüchen und lässt keinen Wunsch unerfüllt. Renommierte Chefköche kreieren Speisen auf Sterne-Niveau, in den extravaganten Spas treffen neueste Behandlungsmethoden ebenso wie jahrtausendealte Traditionen auf müde Muskeln – und machen im Idealfall nicht nur fit für den nächsten Tag, sondern schenken ein Stück Lebensqualität, das den Urlaub überdauert.

Natürlich ist das gebotene Golf für reisende Golfer das Wichtigste. Und auch hier sind die Resorts in diesem Band führend: Ehemalige Spitzenspieler wie Jack Nicklaus, Gary Player und Ray Floyd zeichnen für viele der Courses verantwortlich, Design-Stars wie Pete Dye und Tom Doak konnten ebenfalls in traumhafter Umgebung ihre ondulierten Meisterwerke aus Fairways, Bunkern und Grüns verwirklichen. Einige Resort-Plätze wie Turnberry in Schottland, Teeth of the Dog von Casa de Campo in der Dominikanischen Republik oder Cape Kidnappers in Neuseeland gehören gar zu den schönsten Kursen der Welt und landen auf internationalen Bestenlisten regelmäßig ganz vorne. Plätze wie der K Club haben Sporthistorie geschrieben, und in Stoke Park traten James Bond alias Sean Connery und Auric Goldfinger alias Gert Fröbe zum wohl berühmtesten Matchplay der Filmgeschichte gegeneinander an.

Doch nur wenn der Rahmen stimmt, kommt ein Kunstwerk richtig zur Geltung. Erst wenn auch das Drumherum passt, wird aus der Reise ein unvergessliches Erlebnis. Und der lang anhaltende Erinnerungswert ist bei den hier vorgestellten Golf-Resorts garantiert, denn sie sind in den spektakulärsten Landschaften angesiedelt – vom tropischen Trockenwald bis zur Hochlandwüste, von den Alpen bis zum Mittelmeer, vom Indischen Ozean bis zur Karibik. Golfer können nach der Runde Canyons erkunden, auf alten Indianerpfaden entlangreiten, per Bike oder im Offroader unwegsames Gelände bezwingen, zu Korallenriffen tauchen, den Regenwald aus nächster Nähe bewundern, per Katamaran vor der Küste kreuzen oder auf Safari gehen. Wer eher die Langsamkeit für sich entdecken will, findet in den Resorts private Beach Clubs, Kaminzimmer, Bibliotheken oder Zigarren-Lounges.

Ganzheitlicher Genuss, der weit über die Golfplätze hinausreicht: Das ist das Versprechen, das diese Resorts geben und beschwingt einhalten. Lasst die Spiele beginnen!

Stefan Maiwald

Introduction

Les golfeurs sont de vrais épicuriens. Leurs vacances doivent mettre tous leurs sens en éveil : ils recherchent une intensité, une magnificence, une explosion de couleurs. Le golfeur en voyage affectionne avant tout un bon terrain, mais aussi le verre qui viendra couronner la partie, le spectacle du soleil couchant, le dîner sous un ciel étoilé, et la curiosité de savoir ce que le lendemain pourra bien réserver comme surprise. Les meilleurs complexes hôteliers de golf garantissent de magnifiques parties sur des terrains aussi parfaitement entretenus qu'intelligemment aménagés, et bien plus encore : le service des hôtels présentés comble les demandes les plus exigeantes, ne laissant aucun désir insatisfait. Citons les chefs renommés qui créent des mets dignes de restaurants étoilés, mais aussi les spas qui, dans une ambiance unique, associent les traitements les plus récents aux traditions millénaires dans un seul but : la détente absolue. Ainsi, les golfeurs peuvent pleinement récupérer avant leur journée du lendemain et quittent l'établissement dans un état de bien-être qui perdure longtemps après leurs vacances.

Naturellement, pour les sportifs même amateurs, la qualité des parcours proposés constitue un aspect primordial du voyage. Une fois de plus, les complexes sont exactement dans le ton : bon nombre des terrains ont été conçus par d'anciens joueurs de haut niveau comme Jack Nicklaus, Gary Player et Ray Floyd, ou par les meilleurs architectes, comme Pete Dye et Tom Doak, qui ont réalisé de véritables chefs-d'œuvre dans des décors de rêve en dessinant des fairways aux courbes harmonieuses ponctués de greens et de bunkers. Certains parcours, comme le Turnberry en Écosse, le Teeth of the Dog de Casa de Campo en République dominicaine ou le Cape Kidnappers en Nouvelle-Zélande, comptent parmi les plus beaux du monde et figurent régulièrement aux premiers rangs des classements internationaux. D'autres ont vu s'écrire des pages importantes de l'histoire du sport, comme celui du K Club, ou du cinéma, comme celui de Stoke Park où se sont affrontés James Bond, alias Sean Connery, et Auric Goldfinger, alias Gert Fröbe, pour la partie la plus célèbre du septième art.

Toutefois, pour réaliser un véritable chef-d'œuvre, il faut que le cadre convienne. De même, ce n'est que lorsque le décor est idéal que le voyage devient une expérience inoubliable. Le souvenir des complexes de golf présentés ici perdurera très longtemps, car ils ont été édifiés sur des sites spectaculaires : de la forêt tropicale au désert des hauts plateaux, des Alpes à la Méditerranée, de l'océan Indien à la mer des Caraïbes. Après leur partie, les golfeurs ont la possibilité d'aller à la découverte des canyons, partir à cheval sur les sentiers des Indiens, dompter des pistes impraticables autrement qu'à vélo ou en véhicule tout-terrain, plonger dans les barrières de corail, admirer la forêt tropicale au plus près, longer la côte en catamaran ou faire un safari. Toutefois, certains préfèreront se détendre sur une plage ou se recueillir près de la cheminée d'un salon, d'un fumoir ou d'une bibliothèque.

Un plaisir total qui dépasse largement les limites des fairways : c'est la promesse faite et tenue avec bonheur par ces complexes. Que la partie commence !

Stefan Maiwald

Adare Manor Hotel & Golf Resort

County Limerick, Ireland

In the mid-19th century, one of the oldest clans in Ireland created a country estate with numerous eccentricities: 365 windows (one for each day of the year), 52 chimneys (one for each week), seven columns in the entrance hall (one for each day of the week), and four towers (one for each season). Yet after several generations, the family ran out of money. In 1984, the seventh Earl of Dunraven sold the fairytale estate to a U.S. millionaire of Irish descent, who first converted it into a hotel and then added an 18-hole golf course designed by Robert Trent Jones Senior. Bill Clinton is a welcome guest, and the perfectly groomed parkland course bisected by the River Maigue has hosted the Irish Open twice. Considered one of the most successful opening holes in the world of golf, the first hole is a short par 4 whose green is protected by a winding creek.

Einer der ältesten Clans Irlands erschuf sich Mitte des 19. Jahrhunderts einen Landsitz, der über zahlreiche exzentrische Besonderheiten verfügt: 365 Fenster (für jeden Tag eines), 52 Kamine (für jede Woche einen), sieben Säulen in der Eingangshalle (für jeden Wochentag) und vier Türme (für jede Saison). Doch nach ein paar Generationen ging der Familie das Geld aus; der siebte Earl of Dunraven verkaufte das märchenhafte Anwesen 1984 an einen irischstämmigen US-Millionär, der es zunächst in ein Hotel umwandelte und schließlich mit einem 18-Loch-Platz von Robert Trent Jones Senior veredelte. Bill Clinton ist gern gesehener Gast, und schon zweimal fanden die Irish Open auf dem perfekt manikürten Parkland Course statt, durch den sich der River Maigue zieht. Bereits Bahn 1 – ein kurzes Par 4, dessen Grün von einem Graben verteidigt wird, – gilt als eines der gelungensten Eröffnungslöcher der Golfwelt.

Au milieu du XIXe siècle, l'un des plus anciens clans d'Irlande érigea un bâtiment éclectique pour y installer son siège : 365 fenêtres (une par jour de l'année), 52 cheminées (une par semaine), sept colonnes dans le hall d'entrée (une par jour de la semaine) et quatre tours (une par saison). Mais en 1984, après quelques passages de générations, le manque de fonds obligea l'Earl of Dunraven à vendre le somptueux domaine à un millionnaire américain d'origine irlandaise, qui le transforma d'abord en hôtel avant de le parer d'un parcours 18-trous signé Robert Trent Jones Senior. La rivière Maigue baigne les rives de ce parkland conçu de mains de maître, sur lequel Bill Clinton aime revenir jouer et qui a été choisi à deux reprises pour accueillir l'Irish Open. Le premier trou, un court par 4 dont un fossé protège le green, est connu dans le monde entier pour être l'un des numéros 1 les plus réussis.

Adare Manor Hotel & Golf Resort

Adare, County Limerick
Ireland
T +35 361 605 200, reservations@adaremanor.com
www.adaremanor.com/limerick.html

Rooms: 62 rooms, suites, 2-, 3-, and 4-bedroom townhouses, and 3- and 4-bedroom villas.
Facilities: treatment rooms, indoor heated swimming pool, steam room, fitness room, 2 restaurants, 3 bars, boutique, complimentary parking, boutique, pro shop.
Services: 24 h front desk, concierge, car rental, medical treatment, cookery demonstrations, clay target shooting, whiskey and wine tasting, falconry, complimentary WiFi.
Located: 25 minutes from Shannon International Airport.

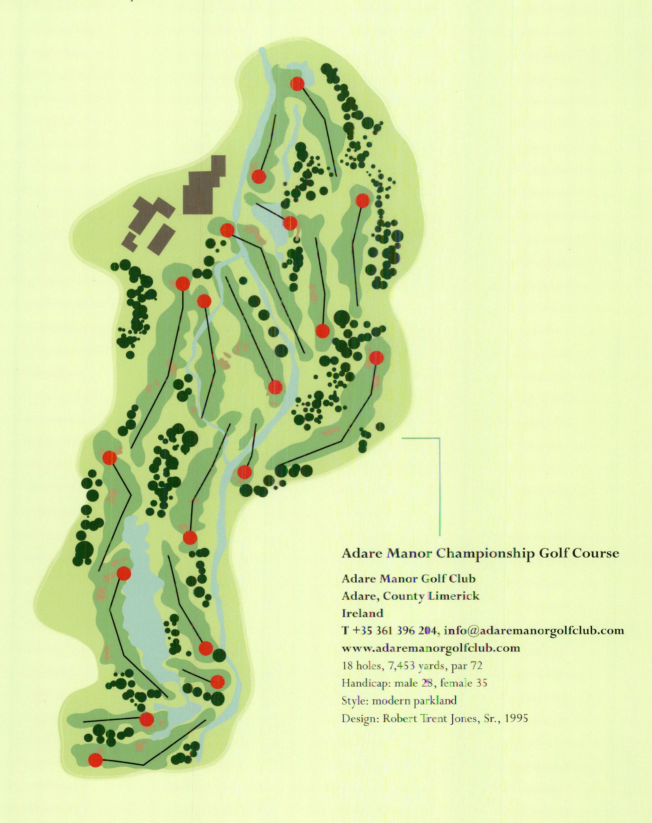

Adare Manor Championship Golf Course

Adare Manor Golf Club
Adare, County Limerick
Ireland
T +35 361 396 204, info@adaremanorgolfclub.com
www.adaremanorgolfclub.com
18 holes, 7,453 yards, par 72
Handicap: male 28, female 35
Style: modern parkland
Design: Robert Trent Jones, Sr., 1995

Dromoland Castle

County Clare, Ireland

The first master of Dromoland ended up on the gallows. Although Donough MacMurrough O'Brien was hanged in Limerick for sedition in 1582, the property remained in the family. The current structure was built in 1835, around the same time as nearby Adare Manor. Also similar to Adare Manor, the family could no longer afford the upkeep of the estate in later years and was finally forced to sell it to an investor. With gently rolling fairways that wind through stands of old trees and around a large lake, the 18-hole golf course is considered to be the Augusta of Ireland, not least because of the outstanding and fast greens. In the ancient regional dialect, Dromoland means "hill of litigation," but the only conflict faced by current guests of the luxury hotel is whether they would prefer to be spoiled at the spa or in the Michelin-star restaurant.

Der erste Herr über Dromoland endete am Galgen. 1582 wurde Donough MacMurrough O'Brien in Limerick wegen umstürzlerischer Umtriebe gehängt. Immerhin blieb das Land in Familienhand, und 1835 wurde der heutige Bau errichtet – praktisch zeitgleich zum nahen und ähnlich prächtigen Adare Manor. Hier wie dort konnte die Adelsfamilie sich den Unterhalt bald nicht mehr leisten und musste an einen Investor verkaufen. Der 18-Loch-Platz, dessen sanft gewellte Fairways sich durch alten Baumbestand und um einen großen See winden, gilt als Irlands Augusta, nicht zuletzt wegen der hervorragenden und blitzschnellen Grüns. Dromoland soll im uralten Dialekt der Gegend „Hügel der Streitigkeiten" bedeuten, doch wer heute das Luxushotel besucht, ringt allenfalls mit sich selbst, ob er sich lieber im Michelin-besternten Hotelrestaurant oder im Spa verwöhnen lassen soll.

Le premier seigneur de Dromoland finit sur la potence : en 1582, Donough MacMurrough O'Brien fut pendu à Limerick pour ses agissements révolutionnaires. Toutefois, les terres restèrent dans la famille. Le bâtiment actuel fut érigé en 1835 – pratiquement au même moment que l'impressionnant Adare Manor situé non loin de là. Ici comme là-bas, la noble famille ne put bientôt plus financer l'entretien et dut vendre à un investisseur. Le parcours 18-trous, dont les fairways doucement ondulés se lovent au milieu d'un ancien espace boisé et cernent un grand lac, est connu pour être l'Augusta d'Irlande notamment pour ses greens aussi rapides que magnifiques. Dromoland signifie en ancien dialecte « colline des litiges ». Pourtant, les visiteurs de l'hôtel n'ont aujourd'hui plus rien à craindre, si ce n'est le dilemme de choisir entre les saveurs du restaurant étoilé et les délicieux soins du spa.

Dromoland Castle

Newmarket-on-Fergus, County Clare
Ireland
T +35 361 368 144 , sales@dromoland.ie
www.dromoland.ie
Rooms: 98 rooms, including 27 suites.
Facilities: pool, sauna, jacuzzi, horse riding, clay shooting, archery, falconry, golf, fishing, tennis, spa, 2 restaurants.
Services: conferences, weddings, children's activities, 24 h room service.
Located: 19 miles (31 kilometers) from Limerick, 20 minutes from Shannon Airport.

Dromoland Castle Golf Course

Dromoland Castle Golf and Country Club
Newmarket-on-Fergus, County Clare
Ireland
+35 361 368 444, golf@dromoland.ie
www.dromoland.ie/golf.html
18 holes, 6,824 yards, par 72,
Handicap: male 28, female 36
Style: traditional parkland
Design: J.B. Carr and Ron Kirby, 1961

Druids Glen Resort

Newtownmountkennedy, Ireland

Two extraordinary golf courses are located to the south of Dublin—and surprisingly enough, they are parkland courses with nary a view of the ocean to be had. Nestled between the two courses is a resort that offers modern luxury without unnecessary flourishes. Planners thankfully chose not to go the route of fake battlements for the new construction, nor did they install gardens that might look out of place. The hotel is a functional interpretation of elegance; here, golf is what matters. Druids Glen winds through a seemingly enchanted woodland landscape, while Druids Heath is a more open golf course where a constant wind affects every swing. Some of the par-3 holes at Druids Glen are among the most beautiful in the world. A perfect place to relax after a round of golf is the Fairways Bar, where patrons can enjoy a good selection of beer and whiskey, and juicy hamburgers will satisfy hearty appetites.

Im Süden Dublins sind zwei Golfplätze der Extraklasse entstanden – und das Erstaunliche daran: Es handelt sich um Parkland Courses, den Blick aufs Meer sucht man vergebens. Mittendrin liegt ein Resort, das modernen Luxus ohne große Schnörkel präsentiert. Auf falsche Zinnen hat man bei dem Neubau dankenswerterweise verzichtet, auch Gartenlandschaften wurden nicht extra künstlich hochgezogen. Das Hotel ist eine funktionale Interpretation von Noblesse; hier ist Golf das Wesentliche. Druids Glen zieht sich durch eine verwunschen wirkende Baumlandschaft, während Druids Heath der offenere Platz ist, auf dem ein ständiger Wind in jeden Schlag eingreift. Einige der Par-3-Löcher von Druids Glen gehören zweifellos zu den hübschesten der Welt. Ein Tipp für die Zeit nach der Runde ist die Golfer-Bar, wo es eine gute Auswahl an Bier und Whiskey und dazu saftige Hamburger für den großen Hunger gibt.

Au sud de Dublin se trouvent deux terrains extraordinaires – et le plus étonnant à cela est qu'il est inutile de chercher la vue sur la mer, il s'agit de deux parcours de type parkland. Le cœur du domaine abrite un complexe moderne offrant un luxe sobre et élégant. Le nouveau bâtiment a judicieusement été construit sans créneaux décoratifs, de la même manière que le jardin qui n'a reçu aucun attribut artificiel. L'hôtel est une représentation fonctionnelle de la notion de noblesse ; le golf constitue l'essence du lieu. Druids Glen s'étend sur un paysage rappelant les forêts enchantées, alors que Druids Heath est le terrain le plus exposé à l'incessant vent qui s'invite à chaque coup. Certains par 3 de Druids Glen appartiennent sans aucun doute aux plus raffinés qui existent. Un conseil pour conclure une session, le bar attend les golfeurs avec une excellente sélection de bière et de whiskey. De plus, de savoureux hamburgers satisferont les plus grands appétits.

Druids Glen Resort

Newcastle Road, Newtownmountkennedy
Ireland
T +35 312 870 800, reservations@druidsglenresort.com
www.druidsglenresort.com
Rooms: 145 rooms and suites.
Facilities: restaurant, bar, parking lot, indoor pool, spa, golf.
Services: 24 h front desk.
Located: 30 minutes from Dublin city center, 37 miles (60 kilometers) from Dublin Airport.

Druids Glen Course

18 holes, 7,046 yards, par 71
Handicap: male 28, female 36
Style: modern parkland
Design: Pat Ruddy and Tom Craddock, 1995

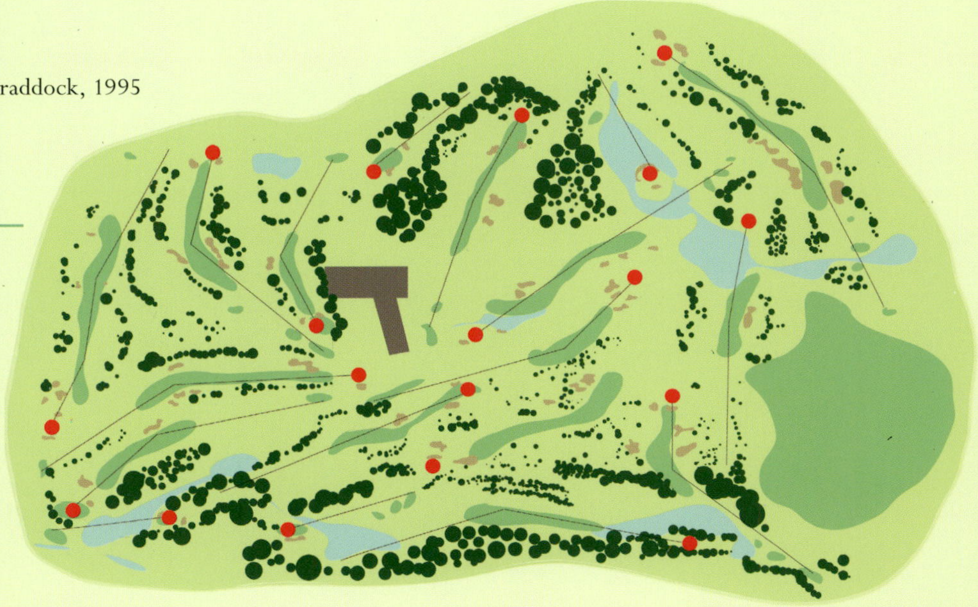

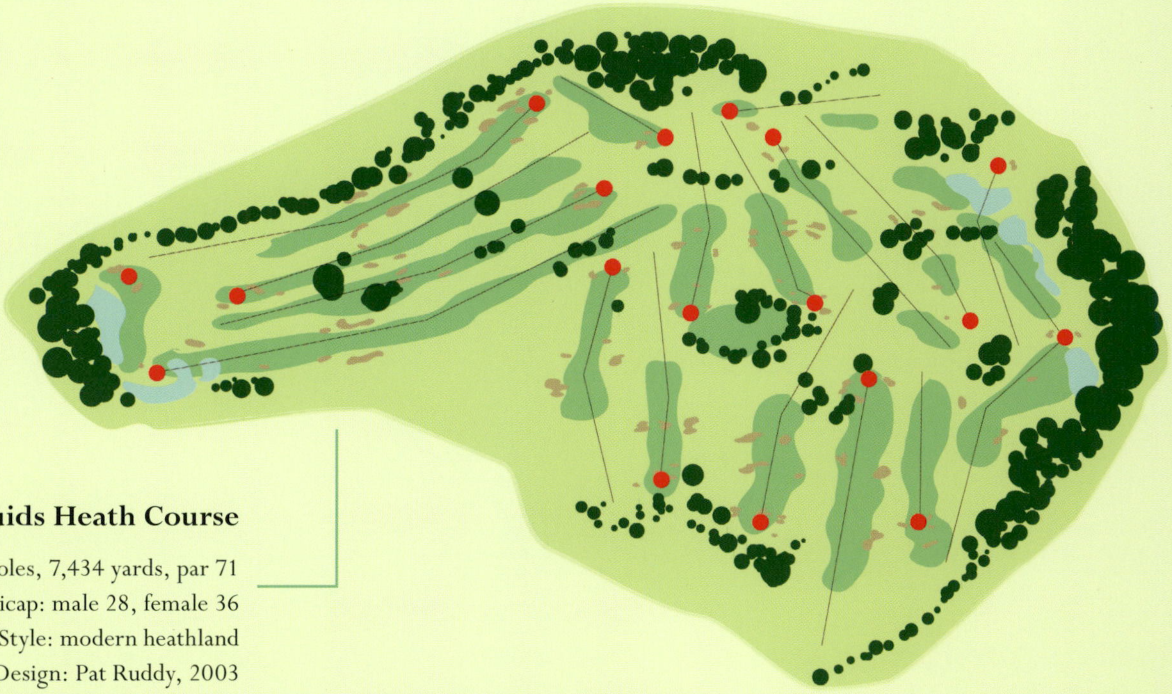

Druids Heath Course

18 holes, 7,434 yards, par 71
Handicap: male 28, female 36
Style: modern heathland
Design: Pat Ruddy, 2003

The K Club

Straffan, Ireland

An unusual name, an unusual project: Michael Smurfit, one of the richest men in Ireland, wanted to build a monument to himself. He has achieved that with the K Club: The K stands for county Kildare. Two Arnold Palmer courses along the bank of the River Liffey leave nothing to be desired, and each has a unique design. One course appeals to golfers with its magnificent parkland design, while the other challenges players with its unusual links elements, dunes, and expansive greens, although the ocean is far away. The Ryder Cup was held on the parkland loop in 2006, for the first time ever in Ireland. Team Europe led by Captain Ian Woosnam won hands down. The dunes course hosted the European Open from 1995 to 2007. Though the resort is only a few years old, the original Straffan House estate was first mentioned in the year 550—it's hard to imagine that any golf hotel in the world can offer more history than that.

Ungewöhnlicher Name, ungewöhnliches Projekt: Michael Smurfit, einer der reichsten Iren, wollte sich ein Denkmal setzen. Das ist ihm mit dem K Club gelungen – das K steht für die Grafschaft Kildare. Zwei Arnold-Palmer-Plätze entlang der hiesigen Ufer der Liffey lassen keine Wünsche offen und sind bewusst ganz unterschiedlich angelegt worden; einer gefällt mit prächtigem Parkland-Design, der andere fordert die Spieler mit ungewöhnlichen Links-Elementen, Dünen und großen Grüns heraus, obwohl das Meer weit entfernt ist. Auf der Parkland-Schleife fand 2006 der Ryder Cup statt, zum ersten Mal überhaupt in Irland. Team Europa mit Kapitän Ian Woosnam gewann haushoch. Von 1995 bis 2007 hatte der Dünenplatz die European Open zu Gast. Zwar ist das Resort erst wenige Jahre alt, das ursprüngliche Anwesen Straffan House ist jedoch schon seit dem Jahr 550 urkundlich belegt – mehr Geschichte kann kein Golfhotel der Welt bieten.

À nom inhabituel, projet non conventionnel : Michael Smurfit, un des hommes les plus riches d'Irlande, voulait un monument à sa propre mémoire. Il a réussi avec le K Club – le K vient de Kildare, le nom du comté. Deux parcours signés Arnold Palmer bordent la rivière Liffey. Forts de leurs conceptions différentes, ils ont de quoi combler les souhaits de tout golfeur. L'un, véritable parkland, séduit par sa réalisation, l'autre met les joueurs au défi avec d'inhabituels éléments de links, des dunes et de vastes greens, bien que la mer soit à plusieurs kilomètres. Le parcours a accueilli en 2006 la Ryder Cup pour sa première édition Irlandaise, que l'équipe européenne emmenée par Ian Woosnam avait remporté haut la main. De 1995 à 2007, c'est sur le parcours dunaire que l'European Open avait élu domicile. Si le complexe n'a que quelques années, la propriété de Straffan House atteste de son occupation dès l'an 550 – aucun autre hôtel-golf au monde ne peut se vanter d'un tel héritage.

The K Club

County Kildare, Straffan
Ireland
T +35 316 017 200, sales@kclub.ie
www.kclub.ie
Rooms: 60 rooms and 9 suites.
Facilities: 3 restaurants, golf, and K Spa.
Services: 24 h room service, weddings.
Located: 40 minutes from Dublin Airport.

The Palmer Ryder Cup Course

18 holes, 7,337 yards, par 72
Handicap: male 28, female 45
Style: modern parkland
Design: Arnold Palmer, 1991

The Palmer Smurfit Course

18 holes, 7,277 yards, par 72
Handicap: male 28, female 45
Style: inland links
Design: Arnold Palmer, 1991

Portmarnock Hotel & Golf Links

Dublin, Ireland

Not far from Dublin, the first hole at this golf resort is a reminder to enjoy life while you can—visible just off to the right is a cemetery with magnificent crosses that has collected its share of golf balls. Portmarnock feels like a course that has been around forever, when in fact it was designed in 1995 by Bernhard Langer, Germany's golf superstar. "I couldn't have designed this kind of classic links course anywhere else," remarked the two-time Masters Champion about his masterpiece with raised tees and greens that has also hosted the Ladies Irish Open. The hotel was once the residence for members of the Jameson Whiskey dynasty, and the fairways mark the spot where James Mollison took off in 1932 on the first east-to-west transatlantic flight. Golfers should plan on finishing off their round in style by stopping by the Jameson Bar and enjoying a glass of Jameson whiskey in honor of the family who founded the estate.

Nur einen entschlossenen Abschlag von Dublin entfernt, gemahnt gleich die erste Bahn daran, das Leben zu genießen, solange noch Zeit bleibt – liegt doch rechter Hand ein Friedhof mit prächtigen Grabkreuzen, die schon den einen oder anderen Ball abbekommen haben. Portmarnock wirkt wie ein uralter Platz, dabei hat ihn Deutschlands Golfstar Bernhard Langer erst 1995 entworfen. „Nirgendwo sonst hätte ich einen so klassischen Links Course bauen können", freut sich der zweimalige Masters-Champion über sein Meisterwerk mit den erhöhten Abschlägen und Grüns, auf dem auch schon die Ladies Irish Open ausgetragen wurden. Das Hotel selbst war einst Residenz der Whiskey-Dynastie Jameson, und von dort, wo sich heute die Fairways entlangziehen, startete 1932 James Mollison zum ersten Ost-West-Flug über den Atlantik. Stilecht sollten Golfer die Runde in der Jameson Bar mit einem Glas Whiskey jener Marke beenden, deren Besitzer das Anwesen errichtet haben.

À portée de club de Dublin, le premier trou de ce golf est déjà une invitation à profiter de la vie tant qu'il en est encore temps – à sa droite se trouve un cimetière où se dressent d'impressionnantes croix qui ont certainement reçu leur lot de balles perdues. Portmarnock donne l'impression d'un parcours centenaire ; il n'a pourtant été tracé qu'en 1995 par le champion allemand Bernhard Langer. « Jamais je n'aurais pu concevoir ailleurs qu'ici un parcours links aussi classique », jubile le double vainqueur des masters en parlant de son chef-d'œuvre – avec ses départs et ses greens surélevés – qui a d'ailleurs déjà accueilli le Ladies Irish Open. L'hôtel, autrefois la résidence de la dynastie du Whiskey Jameson, et les fairways se trouvent à l'endroit même où James Mollison s'était lancé en 1932 pour le premier vol transatlantique est-ouest. Selon la coutume, les golfeurs se doivent de terminer le parcours au Jameson Bar avec un verre de la célèbre marque des fondateurs du domaine.

Portmarnock Hotel & Golf Links

Strand Road, Dublin
Ireland
T +35 318 460 611, info@portmarnock.com
www.portmarnock.com
Rooms: 138 rooms and suites.
Facilities: restaurant, bar, parking lot, golf.
Services: 24 h front desk.
Located: 4 miles (7 kilometers) from Dublin Airport.

The Championship Portmarnock Links Golf Course

18 holes, 6,886 yards, par 71
Handicap: male 28, female 36
Style: links
Design: Bernhard Langer, 1995

The Gleneagles Hotel

Auchterarder, United Kingdom

Nothing left to be desired: Three 18-hole courses and a short 9-hole course await guests eager to tee off. The PGA Centenary Course is the venue for the Ryder Cup in 2014. The holes wind their way around the nearly century-old resort located north of Glasgow and Edinburgh, and the resort's restaurant has garnered gourmet awards for years. With luxurious rooms and well pruned gardens set in a romantic hilly landscape, this resort captures the essence of Scotland. Guests interested in more than golf and dining can enjoy horseback riding, fly fishing, skeet shooting, and numerous other activities typically enjoyed by the landed gentry. Guests can even try their hands at falconry; those brave enough might experience an eagle perched on their leather-clad forearm. And if you feel that your golf game needs some tweaking, look no further than the prestigious PGA National Golf Academy, which has been visited by tour pros from around the world.

Mehr kann sich kein Golfer wünschen: Gleich drei 18-Loch-Plätze sowie ein 9-Loch-Kurzplatz warten auf abschlagwillige Gäste; auf dem PGA Centenary Course wird 2014 zudem der Ryder Cup stattfinden. Die Bahnen ziehen sich um das beinahe hundert Jahre alte Resort nördlich von Glasgow und Edinburgh, dessen Restaurant seit Jahren Gourmet-Preise einheimst. Das Hotel mit seinen prächtigen Räumen und akkurat gepflegten Gartenanlagen in wildromantischer Hügellandschaft wirkt wie die Essenz Schottlands. Wem Golf und Schlemmen noch nicht reichen, der darf sich auch mit Reitausflügen, Fliegenfischen, Tontaubenschießen und allerlei anderen land-adligen Aktivitäten die Zeit vertreiben. Selbst als Falkner kann man sich versuchen; wer mutig ist, bekommt gar einen Adler auf den ledergeschützten Unterarm gesetzt. Und wer an seinem Golfspiel verzweifelt, wendet sich vertrauensvoll an die renommierte PGA National Golf Academy, zu der auch Tour-Profis aus aller Welt pilgern.

Un golfeur ne pourrait rêver mieux : d'entrée de jeu, trois parcours 18-trous ainsi qu'un 9-trous attendent les visiteurs ; le PGA Centenary Course servira d'ailleurs de cadre pour la Ryder Cup en 2014. Le parcours s'étend autour du complexe de presque un siècle situé au nord de Glasgow et Édimbourg. Le restaurant est titulaire de plusieurs distinctions depuis de nombreuses années. Toute l'essence de l'Écosse se retrouve dans cet hôtel avec ses somptueuses chambres et ses jardins au cœur de collines fleurant la passion romantique. Si le golf et la gastronomie ne suffisent plus, la carte des divertissements offre également des sorties équestres, de pêche à la mouche, de tir au pigeon et toutes autres sortes d'activités de gentleman. Il est même possible de s'initier à la fauconnerie ; les courageux pouvant se voir déposer un aigle sur leur avant-bras revêtu de cuir. Les golfeurs voulant se perfectionner peuvent se tourner en toute confiance vers la célèbre PGA National Golf Academy, où accourent aussi les professionnels du monde entier.

The Gleneagles Hotel

PH3 1NF Auchterarder
United Kingdom
T +44 176 4662 231, resort.sales@gleneagles.com
www.gleneagles.com
Rooms: 232 rooms and suites.
Facilities: spa, indoor spa pool, parking lot, golf, tennis courts, 4 restaurants, bar.
Services: 24 h front desk, car rental.
Located: 1 hour from Glasgow and Edinburgh International Airports.

The PGA Centenary Course

18 holes, 6,815 yards, par 73
Handicap: not specific
Style: moorland
Design: Jack Nicklaus, 1993

The King's Course

18 holes, 6,125 yards, par 71
Handicap: not specific
Style: moorland
Design: James Braid, 1919

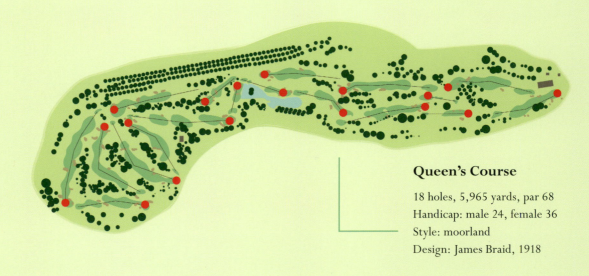

Queen's Course

18 holes, 5,965 yards, par 68
Handicap: male 24, female 36
Style: moorland
Design: James Braid, 1918

The Grove

Hertfordshire, United Kingdom

The "landed gentry" feeling begins just a few minutes outside of London. The estate was built in 1703, and explorer James Cook gave the owners the seeds to the walnut tree that still shades the terrace today. The illustrious guest list of this exclusive hotel includes names such as Queen Victoria, Horace Walpole, and Lord Palmerston. In 2006, Tiger Woods won the World Golf Championships on the adjacent golf course. In his victory, Woods had little difficulty with the undulating fairways and lightning-swift greens—he achieved the unheard-of score of 23 under par, eight strokes better than runners-up Adam Scott and Ian Poulter. "One of the best courses I've ever played on," he was reported to have said afterwards. In addition, Woods set a very special record: On the 18th hole (now the 9th) he played an eagle three days in a row.

Nur wenige Minuten außerhalb von London beginnt das Landlord-Gefühl. Schon 1703 wurde das Anwesen errichtet, und Weltumsegler James Cook schenkte dem Besitzer die Samen zu jenem Walnussbaum, der noch heute der Terrasse Schatten spendet. Die illustre Gästeliste des Nobelhotels enthält Namen wie Queen Victoria, Horace Walpole und Lord Palmerston. Tiger Woods gewann 2006 die World Golf Championships auf dem angrenzenden Platz. Woods hatte bei seinem Sieg wenig Mühe mit den ondulierten Fairways und pfeilschnellen Grüns – er schaffte den Fabelscore von 23 Schlägen unter Par, acht Schläge besser als die zweitplatzierten Adam Scott und Ian Poulter. „Einer der besten Plätze, die ich je gespielt habe", gab er anschließend zu Protokoll. Außerdem stellte Woods einen ganz besonderen Rekord auf: An der 18 (der heutigen 9) spielte er drei Tage hintereinander ein Eagle.

À quelques minutes de Londres, il est possible de se mettre dans la peau d'un lord anglais. Pour cela, il suffit de se rendre au Grove, domaine créé en 1703, dont le propriétaire reçut des mains du navigateur James Cook les graines du noyer dont l'ombre couvre aujourd'hui la terrasse. Au nombre des illustres pensionnaires de l'hôtel s'ajoutent la reine Victoria, Horace Walpole et Lord Palmerston. Plus récemment, en 2006, Tiger Woods a remporté sur le parcours attenant les World Golf Championships. Les fairways ondulés et les greens rapides n'avaient causé que peu de soucis au golfeur américain : il avait obtenu le fabuleux score de 23 sous le par, soit huit de moins que les deuxièmes Adam Scott et Ian Poulter. « C'est l'un des meilleurs parcours sur lesquels j'aie joué », a-t-il confessé à l'issue de la cérémonie. De plus, Woods a établi un record bien particulier : sur le 18 (aujourd'hui le 9), il a réalisé un eagle trois jours d'affilée.

The Grove

Chandler's Cross, WD3 4TG Hertfordshire
United Kingdom
T +44 192 3807 807, reservations@thegrove.co.uk
www.thegrove.co.uk

Rooms: 217 rooms, including 16 suites.
Facilities: 3 restaurants, 3 bars, private park, inside and outside pool, spa, gym, golf, tennis courts.
Services: 24 h front desk, kids club.
Located: 30 minutes from London city center and Heathrow Airport.

The Grove Golf Course

18 holes, 6,153 yards, par 71
Style: classic parkland
Design: Kyle Phillips, 2003

Stoke Park

Buckinghamshire, United Kingdom

A true star—no other golf course has played as big a role in movie history as Stoke Park. It was the setting for the first encounter between James Bond (Sean Connery) and Auric Goldfinger (Gert Fröbe) when they play a high-stakes game for a bar of gold. The match ends when Bond cheats his way to victory, but Goldfinger's manservant Oddjob has the last word when he severs the head of a statue with a deft throw of his steel-rimmed bowler. In later years, scenes from the 18th Bond movie "Tomorrow Never Dies" and "Bridget Jones's Diary" were filmed here as well. But the 27-hole course west of London is a must for more than movie fans: In 1908, famed designer Harry Colt created a timeless jewel in over 345 acres of forest and parkland. The difficult 16th hole of Augusta, the telling location for so many US Masters games, was modeled after the 7th hole at Stoke Park with its water hazard to the left of the green.

Der Club ist ein echter Star – kein anderer Golfplatz hat so sehr Filmgeschichte geschrieben wie Stoke Park. Hier trafen James Bond alias Sean Connery und Auric Goldfinger alias Gert Fröbe das erste Mal aufeinander und spielten um einen Barren Gold. Das Match endete mit einem (erschummelten) Sieg des britischen Agenten, aber Goldfingers Gehilfe Oddjob hatte das letzte Wort, indem er mit seiner scharfen Melone eine Statue köpfte. Später sollten auch noch Szenen des 18. Bond-Films „Der Morgen stirbt nie" sowie „Bridget Jones" hier gedreht werden. Doch nicht nur für Cineasten ist der 27-Loch-Platz westlich von London ein Muss: Der berühmte Designer Harry Colt hat im Jahr 1908 ein zeitloses Juwel in 140 Hektar Wald und Flur erschaffen. Die siebte Bahn von Stoke Park mit ihrem Wasserhindernis links am Grün war das Vorbild für das schwierige 16. Loch von Augusta, an dem sich so manches US Masters entscheidet.

Le club est une véritable vedette – aucun autre terrain de golf n'a écrit l'histoire du cinéma comme celui de Stoke Park. Pour leur première rencontre, James Bond, alias Sean Connery, et Auric Goldfinger, alias Gert Fröbe, y jouèrent un lingot d'or. Le match se solda par une victoire (faussée) de l'agent britannique, mais Oddjob, le domestique de Goldfinger, eut le dernier mot en tranchant la tête d'une statue à l'aide de son chapeau melon. Quelques années plus tard, des scènes du 18e James Bond « Demain ne meurt jamais » et de « Bridget Jones » y furent tournées. Pourtant, le terrain de 27 trous à l'ouest de Londres n'est pas seulement un must pour les cinéastes : le célèbre architecte Harry Colt a créé en 1908 un joyau hors du temps au milieu de 140 hectares de forêts et de champs. Le trou numéro 7 de Stoke Park avec son obstacle d'eau à gauche du green a servi de modèle pour le difficile numéro 16 d'Augusta, un trou souvent décisif à l'US Masters.

Stoke Park

Park Road, SL2 4PG Stoke Poges, Buckinghamshire
United Kingdom
T +44 175 3717 171, info@stokepark.com
www.stokepark.com
Rooms: 49 rooms and suites.
Facilities: spa, gym, tennis courts, golf, restaurant, bar.
Services: 24 h front desk, parking lot.
Located: 8 miles (13 kilometers) from Heathrow Airport, 30 minutes from London Central Station.

"Stoke Poges"
27-hole Championship Golf Course

27 holes (9-hole courses Colt, Alison, Lane Jackson)
6,751 yards (Colt/Alison), par 71
6,302 yards (Alison/Lane Jackson), Par 71
6,569 yards (Colt/Lane Jackson), Par 72
Handicap: male 28, female 36
Style: traditional parkland
Design: Harry Shapland Colt, 1908

Turnberry Resort

Turnberry, United Kingdom

The Ailsa Course at Turnberry is one of the most beautiful courses in Scotland. In World War II, however, even the golfing world made sacrifices when the fairways were turned into airstrips for Allied fighter planes—some of those leveled areas are still visible today. The view of the Irish Sea and the white lighthouse almost distract from the incredible holes—such as the difficult 10th hole with its island sand bunker. 10,000 spectators witnessed golf history being made here in July 2009 when Tom Watson, already 59 at the time, nearly won his sixth British Open. Although the resort's second 18-hole course, the Kintyre, is overshadowed by its older brother, it has its own unique appeal thanks to its often dramatic changes in elevation and tricky greens. Every afternoon at five o'clock, a bagpiper plays on the steps of the resort to greet returning golfers. The rooms located at the front of the resort have a stunning view of the golf course and the Irish Sea.

Der Ailsa Course von Turnberry gilt als einer der schönsten Plätze Schottlands, doch im Zweiten Weltkrieg musste auch die Golfwelt Opfer bringen. Die Fairways wurden zu Start- und Landepisten für alliierte Jagdflugzeuge umgebaut. Noch heute sind einige planierte Flächen zu sehen. Der Blick auf die Irische See und den weißen Leuchtturm lenkt beinahe von den großartigen Bahnen ab, etwa der schwierigen 10 mit ihrem Insel-Sandbunker. Im Juli 2009 erlebten hier zehntausende Zuschauer Golfgeschichte, als der schon 59-jährige Tom Watson beinahe seine sechste British Open gewinnen konnte. Der zweite 18-Loch-Platz namens Kintyre steht im Schatten seines älteren Bruders, hat aber mit seinen oft dramatischen Höhenunterschieden und trickreichen Grüns einen ganz eigenen Reiz. Auf den Stufen des Resorts, von dessen Zimmern der Blick über den Platz und die Irische See schweift, begrüßt jeden Tag um 17 Uhr ein Dudelsackspieler die heimkehrenden Golfer.

Ailsa Course à Turnberry est connu pour être l'un des plus beaux parcours d'Écosse. Pourtant, ce haut lieu du golf a lui aussi souffert de la Seconde Guerre mondiale. Les allées avaient été transformées en pistes pour le décollage et l'atterrissage des avions de chasse alliés. Quelques surfaces planes témoignent d'ailleurs encore de cette époque. La vue sur la mer d'Irlande et le phare blanc qui la domine s'efforcent de ravir la vedette à un parcours beau et exigeant, à l'image du trou numéro 10 et de son bunker. En juillet 2009, dix mille spectateurs ont pu vivre un moment historique lorsque Tom Watson, 59 ans, a frôlé ce qui aurait été sa sixième victoire au British Open. Le deuxième 18-trous, appelé Kintyre, vit dans l'ombre de son frère aîné, mais propose un tout autre caractère avec ses forts dénivelés et ses greens capricieux. Chaque jour à 17 heures, un joueur de cornemuse s'installe sur les marches de l'hôtel pour saluer le retour des golfeurs vers leurs chambres qui donnent sur les terrains et la mer.

Turnberry Resort

Maidens Road, KA26 9LT Turnberry
United Kingdom
T +44 165 5331 000, turnberry@luxurycollection.com
www.turnberryresort.co.uk

Rooms: 150 rooms and suites, including self-catering lodges and apartments.
Facilities: golf courses, 5 restaurants, bars, spa, indoor pool, gym.
Services: resort shuttles, hotel valet, 24 h front desk, transportation services.
Located: 45 minutes from Prestwick Airport.

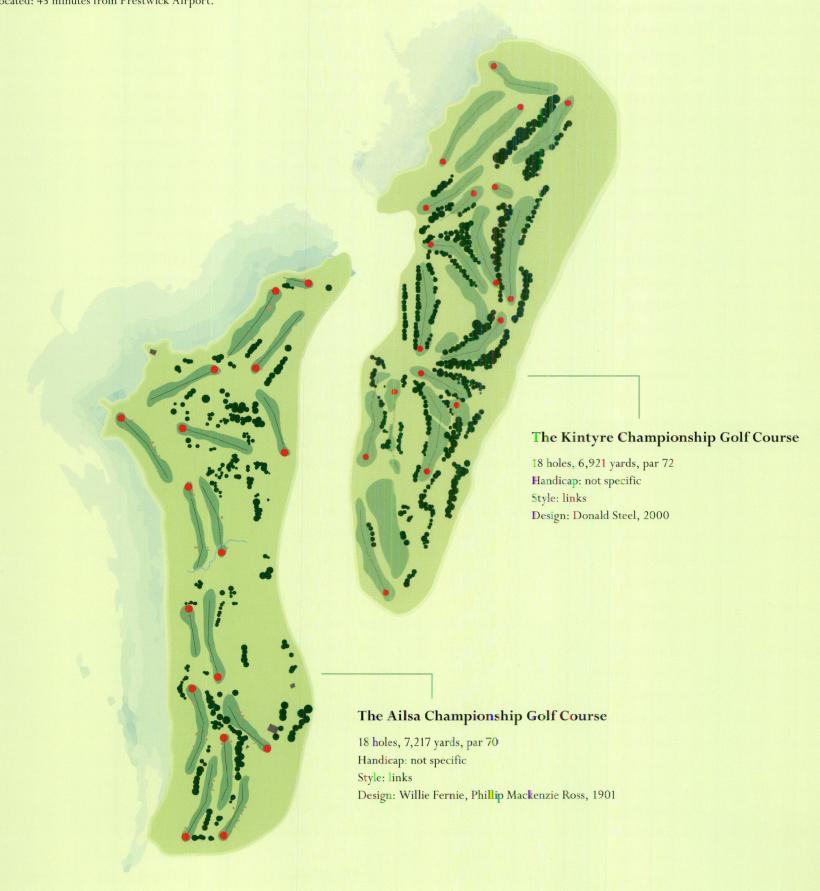

The Kintyre Championship Golf Course

18 holes, 6,921 yards, par 72
Handicap: not specific
Style: links
Design: Donald Steel, 2000

The Ailsa Championship Golf Course

18 holes, 7,217 yards, par 70
Handicap: not specific
Style: links
Design: Willie Fernie, Phillip Mackenzie Ross, 1901

Grand Resort Bad Ragaz

Bad Ragaz, Switzerland

Spring water gushes from the Tamina Gorge. The warm thermal water forms the heart of what is likely the poshest hotel in Switzerland—a country where there is no shortage of competition when it comes to luxury accommodations. Located to the south of St. Gallen, Grand Resort Bad Ragaz boasts extensive grounds. Guests find Swiss elegance at every turn, from the gourmet restaurant Äbtestube, to the 59,000-square-foot spa, to the 18-hole golf course at Bad Ragaz. Over 100 years old, this course is the venue for numerous professional tournaments, and its mature woodlands call for strategy instead of wild drives. Recently added Heidiland is a 9-hole course which features a large Golf Academy and fantastic training possibilities. If you would like to explore the picturesque area surrounding Bad Ragaz, you can do so in the most relaxing way imaginable: On hand at the Grand Resort are Mercedes limousines with chauffeurs.

Aus der Taminaschlucht sprudelt es äußerst ertragreich. Das warme Thermalwasser bildet die Grundlage für das wohl nobelste Hotel der Schweiz – einem Land, in dem die Konkurrenz an Luxusherbergen bekanntlich nicht klein ist. Das Grand Resort Bad Ragaz südlich von St. Gallen ist eingebettet in eine weitläufige Parklandschaft. Schweizer Eleganz finden Gäste beispielsweise im Gourmetrestaurant Äbtestube, dem 5 500 Quadratmeter großen Spa und dem mehr als 100 Jahre alten 18-Loch-Platz von Bad Ragaz, einem Schauplatz zahlreicher Profiturniere, dessen alter Baumbestand taktisches Spiel statt wilder Drives erfordert. Vor wenigen Jahren kam der 9-Loch-Platz Heidiland hinzu, der zudem eine große Golf-Akademie und traumhafte Trainingsmöglichkeiten offeriert. Wer die malerische Gegend rund um Bad Ragaz erkunden will, kann das auf sehr entspannte Art tun: Das Grand Resort hält Mercedes-Limousinen mit Chauffeur bereit.

Les eaux qui jaillissent des gorges de la Tamina sont particulièrement bénéfiques. L'eau chaude thermale constitue l'essence de l'hôtel sans doute le plus noble de Suisse – un pays pourtant réputé pour ne pas manquer de logements de luxe. Le Grand Resort Bad Ragaz situé au sud de Saint-Gall se niche au cœur d'un vaste parc à l'anglaise. L'élégance helvète se retrouve notamment dans le restaurant gastronomique Äbtestube, le spa de 5 500 mètres carrés et le parcours de golf centenaire de 18 trous de Bad Ragaz, terrain de jeu de nombreux joueurs professionnels, dont l'ancien espace boisé exige plus un sens affûté de la stratégie qu'un puissant drive. Depuis quelques années, l'offre s'est enrichie du 9-trous Heidiland associé à une académie de golf et à de merveilleuses installations d'entraînement. Pour les clients désireux de découvrir les environs pittoresques du domaine, il existe une solution très reposante : l'hôtel met à disposition des limousines Mercedes avec chauffeur.

Grand Resort Bad Ragaz

Pfäferserstrasse 8, CH-7310 Bad Ragaz
Switzerland
T +41 813 033 030, reservation@resortragaz.ch
www.resortragaz.ch
Rooms: 290 rooms and suites.
Facilities: restaurant, bar, spa, tennis court, golf, outdoor pool, parking lot, casino, rooms for disabled.
Services: 24 h front desk, car rental, medical treatment.
Located: 62 miles (100 kilometers) from Bodensee-Airport Friedrichshafen and Zurich Airport.

Golf Club Bad Ragaz

Hans-Albrecht-Strasse, CH-7310 Bad Ragaz
Switzerland
T +41 813 033 717, golfclub@resortragaz.ch
www.golfclubragaz.ch

Golf Club Heidiland

Maienfelderstrasse 50, CH-7310 Bad Ragaz
Switzerland
+41 813 033 700, gcheidiland@resortragaz.ch
www.gcheidiland.ch

18-hole PGA Championship Course

18 holes, 6,241 yards (5,707 meters), par 70
Handicap: 30
Style: tree-lined parkland
Design: Donald Harradine, 1905

9-hole Executive Course

9 holes, 1,989 yards (1,819 meters), par 31
Handicap: 50
Style: flat countryside parkland
Design: Peter Harradine, 2006

Palazzo Arzaga Hotel Spa & Golf Resort
Calvagese della Riviera, Italy

Located a bit over a mile west of Lake Garda, a 15th-century monastery was recently renovated and converted into a luxury golf resort. The location is so steeped in history that the hotel has been designated a national monument; in fact, some of the suites feature centuries-old frescos. To the right of the entrance, in the San Martino Chapel, golfers can pray for heavenly support—which could come in handy on the 18-hole golf course designed by Jack Nicklaus II. Yet even the 9-hole course designed by South African golf legend Gary Player is tricky. Players can enjoy the magnificent view from the raised tee for the 18th hole—but they would be wise to keep the water hazard to the left of the fairway in mind. After a round of golf, players can pay a visit to the spa and then wind up the evening at restaurant Il Moretto, where they can peruse an exquisite wine list in the warm light cast by wrought-iron chandeliers.

Ein paar Kilometer westlich vom Gardasee liegt ein Kloster aus dem 15. Jahrhundert, das vor einigen Jahren zum luxuriösen Golfresort umgebaut wurde. Der Ort erweist sich als so geschichtsträchtig, dass das Hotel als nationales Monument gilt. In einigen Suiten sind noch jahrhundertealte Fresken erhalten, und rechts vom Eingang, in der Kapelle San Martino, können Golfer um himmlischen Beistand bitten, der auf den 18 Bahnen des Platzes von Jack Nicklaus II. nicht schaden kann; doch auch der 9-Loch-Platz der südafrikanischen Golflegende Gary Player ist trickreich. Einen prächtigen Blick genießen Spieler vom erhöhten Abschlag der 18 – aber das Wasserhindernis links vom Fairway sollte ebenfalls beachtet werden. Nach der Runde empfiehlt sich ein Besuch im Spa, um anschließend im Restaurant Il Moretto den Tag unter schmiedeeisernen Kronleuchtern und begleitet von der gut sortierten Weinkarte ausklingen zu lassen.

Quelques kilomètres séparent le lac de Garde d'un monastère du XVe siècle, transformé il y a quelques années en un luxueux complexe de golf. Le lieu représente un tel patrimoine que l'hôtel est classé monument historique. D'ailleurs les murs de certaines suites sont parés de fresques centenaires. À droite de l'entrée, les golfeurs peuvent se rendre dans la chapelle San Martino et prier pour mettre les divines chances de leur côté afin de réussir cet exigeant 18-trous conçu par Jack Nicklaus II ; même le 9-trous de la légende sud-africaine Gary Player n'est pas évident. Le départ surélevé du numéro 18 offre aux joueurs une vue splendide – mais attention à l'obstacle d'eau à gauche du fairway. À la fin du circuit, une visite au spa est plus que recommandée avant de terminer la journée au restaurant Il Moretto avec ses lustres en fer forgé et sa riche carte des vins.

Palazzo Arzaga Hotel Spa & Golf Resort

Via Arzaga, 1, 25080 Calvagese della Riviera
Italy
T +39 030 680 600, reservation@palazzoarzaga.com
www.palazzoarzaga.com
Rooms: 84 rooms and suites.
Facilities: 2 restaurants, 2 bars, spa, outdoor and indoor pool, gym, free car park, bicycle rental.
Services: 24 h concierge service, private transfer to and from the airports, cars and limousine service, babysitting.
Located: 25 miles (40 kilometers) from Verona Catullo Airport, 2.5 miles (4 kilometers) from Lake Garda.

Arzaga Golf Club

Via Arzaga, 1, 25080 Calvagese della Riviera
Italy
T +39 030 6806 266, golf@palazzoarzaga.com

Jack Nicklaus II Course

18 holes, 6,850 yards, par 72
Handicap: 34
Style: open parkland
Design: Jack Nicklaus II, 1998

Gary Player Course

9 holes, 2,659 yards, par 36
Handicap: 34
Style: heathland
Design: Gary Player, 1989

Borgo Egnazia Hotel Ville Spa Golf

Savelletri di Fasano, Italy

Apulia is the most underappreciated region in Italy, but Borgo Egnazia just might change that. Opened in 2010, this luxury resort sets standards for Southern Italy and beyond. White is the dominant color, which provides for an impressively clear atmosphere. The resort's Arabian gardens feature palms, jasmine, and prickly pear cacti. Part of the resort and nestled between the hotel and the ocean, the San Domenico Golf Club is one of the most exciting golf courses in all of Italy. Architects carefully designed the course to give players a view of the ocean from every tee and green, and fairways are flanked by spectacular, centuries-old olive trees. Hugh Grant is spotted here several times a year. At the end of each golf season, the Challenge Tour final is held here—one of the most dramatic tournaments in Europe because it determines which of the many young stars can play in the following year's European Tour.

Apulien ist die meistunterschätzte Region Italiens, doch Borgo Egnazia könnte das ändern. Erst 2010 eröffnet, setzt das Luxusresort nicht nur für den Süden des Landes Maßstäbe. Weiß ist die dominierende Farbe, was für eine beeindruckend klare Atmosphäre sorgt. In den arabischen Gärten des Resorts wachsen Palmen, Jasmin und Kaktusfeigen. Der zum Hotel gehörende San Domenico Golf Club zwischen Domizil und Meer ist einer der aufregendsten Plätze des Landes. Die Architekten konstruierten ihn so, dass man von jedem Abschlag und jedem Grün das Meer sieht, und die Fairways werden von spektakulär verwachsenen Olivenbäumen flankiert, die mehrere hundert Jahre alt sind. Hugh Grant wird hier mehrmals im Jahr gesichtet. Am Ende jeder Golfsaison findet auf dem Platz das Finale der Challenge Tour statt, eines der dramatischsten Turniere Europas – entscheidet es doch, wer von den vielen jungen Stars im Folgejahr auf der European Tour spielen darf.

La région des Pouilles compte parmi les moins appréciées d'Italie, mais Borgo Egnazia pourrait y remédier. À peine ouvert en 2010, ce luxueux complexe établit une nouvelle référence au moins pour le sud du pays et probablement au-delà. Le blanc qui domine produit une atmosphère de clarté éblouissante. Les jardins orientaux abritent palmiers, jasmins et figuiers de barbarie. Le San Domenico Golf Club, situé entre la mer et l'hôtel auquel il appartient, offre l'un des parcours les plus excitants du pays. Les architectes l'ont conçu de telle sorte que tous les départs et les greens s'ouvrent sur la mer et que des oliviers centenaires aux troncs spectaculaires bordent les fairways. Hugh Grant s'y rend d'ailleurs à plusieurs reprises chaque année. En fin de chaque saison, le parcours accueille la finale du Challenge Tour, un tournoi comptant parmi les plus relevés d'Europe – tremplin décisif pour de nombreux jeunes champions espérant être invités l'année suivante sur l'European Tour.

Borgo Egnazia Hotel Ville Spa Golf

Contrada Masciola, 72010 Savelletri di Fasano
Italy
T +39 802 255 000, info@borgoegnazia.com
www.borgoegnazia.com/en
Rooms: 184 rooms.
Facilities: 5 restaurants, 4 bars, spa, 18-hole golf course, pool, indoor pool, gym, bicycle rental.
Services: 24 h front desk.
Located: 34 miles (55 kilometers) from Bari Airport, 31 miles (50 kilometers) from Brindisi Airport.

San Domenico Golf

72010 Savelletri di Fasano
Italy
T +39 804 829 200, info@sandomenicogolf.com
www.golfpuglia.it/en/index

The San Domenico Course

18 holes, 7,016 yards, par 72
Handicap: 36
Style: inland link at rocky seaside
Design: European Golf Design, 2000

Marbella Club Hotel, Golf Resort & Spa

Marbella, Spain

This is the place that made the Costa del Sol a hot spot for the jet set. Prince Alfonso von Hohenlohe, an old school playboy, put down his roots in Marbella in the 1950s and bought an old finca right on the Mediterranean. The throngs of guests grew from summer to summer, giving rise to the legendary Marbella Club where the parties didn't end until the sun came up. The club has now turned into a magnificent hotel with a Thalasso spa. Although the club's golf course is 20 minutes away, the design by Dave Thomas more than makes up for the drive. Long distances between the playing groups and views of Gibraltar provide for a relaxing round of golf. Back at the hotel, care is taken to preserve Alfonso's vision of luxury: "Privacy with gardens," was the motto of the bon vivant. At the hotel's Beach Club, guests can take a dip in the heated seawater pool or swim in the ocean and then enjoy champagne and oysters at the buffet.

Hier begann er, der Aufstieg der Costa del Sol zum Jetset-Hotspot. Prinz Alfonso von Hohenlohe, ein Playboy alter Schule, siedelte in den 50er Jahren nach Marbella um und kaufte sich eine alte Finca direkt am Mittelmeer. Die Gästeschar wurde von Sommer zu Sommer größer, bis der legendäre Marbella Club entstand, dessen Partys immer erst endeten, wenn die Sonne aufging. Nun ist aus dem Club ein prächtiges Hotel mit Thalasso-Spa geworden. Der dazugehörige Golfplatz liegt zwar 20 Minuten entfernt, aber das Dave-Thomas-Design entschädigt für die Anfahrt. Lange Abstände zwischen den Flights und Blicke auf Gibraltar sorgen für eine entspannte Golfrunde. Zurück im Hotel wird Alfonsos Vision von Luxus gepflegt: „Privatsphäre mit Gärten" lautete das Motto des Bonvivants. Im Beach Club des Hotels schwimmen Gäste im beheizten Meerwasserpool oder direkt im Meer und stärken sich mit Champagner und Austern am Büfett.

Voici l'établissement qui propulsé la Costa del Sol vers les sommets de la jet-set. Dans les années 50, le Prince Alfonso von Hohenlohe, un play-boy de la vieille école, s'est installé dans une ancienne finca donnant directement sur la Méditerranée. Le nombre de clients ne cessant de croître chaque été, il fallut ouvrir le légendaire Marbella Club où les fêtes ne s'achevaient qu'au lever du soleil. Ce somptueux hôtel abrite un centre de thalassothérapie ; le golf qui lui appartient est certes situé à 20 minutes, mais le projet signé Dave Thomas vous fait vite oublier le trajet : les longs intervalles entre les joueurs et la vue sur Gibraltar garantissent une séance des plus apaisantes. De retour à l'hôtel, la vision du luxe de l'épicurien Alfonso est bien conservée : « un espace privé avec jardin ». Le club de plage de l'hôtel soigne au champagne et aux huîtres les clients après leur bain dans la piscine d'eau de mer chauffée ou dans la Méditerranée.

Marbella Club Hotel, Golf Resort & Spa

Bulevar Principe Alfonso von Hohenlohe, 29600 Marbella
Spain
T +34 952 822 211, hotel@marbellaclub.com
www.marbellaclub.com

Rooms: 84 rooms, 37 suites, and 14 villas.
Facilities: private garden and pools, 6 restaurants, golf, horse riding, spa.
Services: kids club during summer season.
Located: 1 hour from Málaga Airport Pablo Ruiz Picasso.

Marbella Club Golf Resort

Km 3.7, Carreterra de Benahavis, 29679, Benahavis, Marbella
Spain
T +34 952 880 608, reserve.golf@marbellaclub.com
www.marbellaclubgolf.com

El Higueral Golf Course

9 holes, 2,313 yards, par 36
Handicap: male 28, female 36
Style: parkland with lakes
Design: Roderick Bastard, 2008

Marbella Club Golf Course

18 holes, 6,407 yards, par 72
Handicap: male 28, female 36
Style: parkland with lakes
Design: Dave Thomas, 1999

PGA Catalunya Resort

Caldes de Malavella, Spain

A work of art on the Costa Brava: Two wonderful championship golf courses frame a 149-room hotel resort whose elegantly minimalist architecture and panoramic views of the golf course provide plenty of breathing room. The clubhouse, designed by Francisco and Damián Ribas, fits in perfectly with the hotel and resort landscape. The European Tour regularly holds qualification tournaments on the Stadium Course and Tour Course, during which the stars of tomorrow compete for places on the main tour. The Spanish Open, so rich in tradition, has also been held here. Hole 13—a short par 4 on the Stadium Course that features an immediate drop from the tee with a green almost completely surrounded by water—is regarded as one of the most well-made holes of golf in the world. The resort to the south of Girona features a spectacular spa and pool landscape to soothe the weary muscles of golfers.

Ein Kunstwerk an der Costa Brava: Zwei großartige Meisterschaftsplätze umrahmen ein Hotelresort mit 149 Zimmern, dessen reduziert-elegante Architektur und Panoramablick über die Golfbahnen viel Luft zum Atmen lässt. Das Clubhaus, entworfen von Francisco und Damián Ribas, fügt sich perfekt in die Hotel- und Resort-landschaft ein. Die European Tour veranstaltet auf dem Stadium Course und dem Tour Course regelmäßig ihre Qualifikationsturniere, bei denen die Stars von morgen um ihre Plätze auf der Haupttour wetteifern. Auch die traditionsreichen Spanish Open waren schon zu Gast. Bahn 13 – ein kurzes Par 4 auf dem Stadium Course, das vom Abschlag bergab geht und dessen Grün fast komplett von Wasser umschlossen ist – gilt als eine der gelungensten Golfbahnen der Welt. Das Resort im Süden Gironas wartet außerdem mit einer exklusiven Spa- und Poollandschaft auf, in der sich müde Golfermuskeln regenerieren.

Un chef-d'œuvre sur la Costa Brava : deux magnifiques parcours de championnat entourent un complexe de 149 chambres à l'élégante architecture minimaliste, qui offre une vue panoramique sur les parcours et un espace infini. Le clubhouse créé par Francisco et Damián Ribas s'intègre parfaitement dans le paysage. L'European Tour organise régulièrement ses tournois de qualification sur les parcours Stadium Course et Tour Course, lors desquels les champions de demain se disputent les places pour le circuit principal. De plus, le domaine a déjà accueilli le traditionnel Spanish Open. Le trou numéro 13 du Stadium Course – un par 4 entièrement en côte dont le green est presque totalement entouré d'eau – est connu pour être l'un des plus réussis du monde. Le complexe catalan au sud de Gérone abrite un spectaculaire spa avec piscine où se revigorent les golfeurs et leurs muscles durement sollicités.

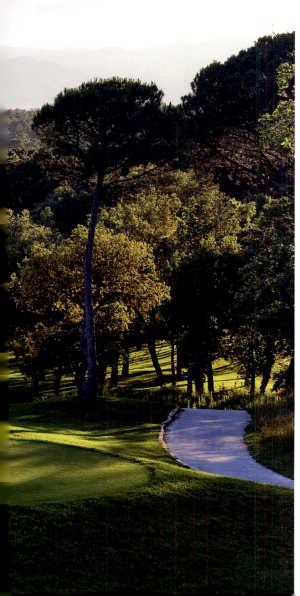

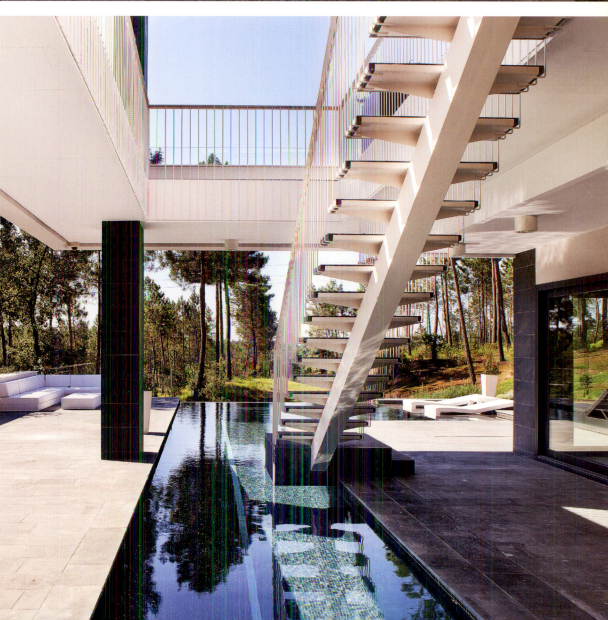

PGA Catalunya Resort

Carretera N-II Km 701, 17455 Caldes de Malavella
Spain
T +34 972 472 577, info@pgacatalunya.com
www.pgacatalunya.com
Rooms: 149 rooms.
Facilities: spa, indoor and outdoor pools, jacuzzi and saunas, tennis, Quimera fine-dining restaurant, Tast brasserie restaurant, lobby bar, 36Bar,
Bistrot restaurant, pro shop.
Services: 24 h security.
Located: 4 miles (6 kilometers) from Girona Airport, 62 miles (100 kilometers) from Barcelona Airport El Prat.

PGA Catalunya Tour Course

18 holes, 6,065 yards, par 72
Handicap: male 28, female 36
Style: modern parkland
Design: Angel Gallardo and Neil Coles with
European Golf Design, 2005

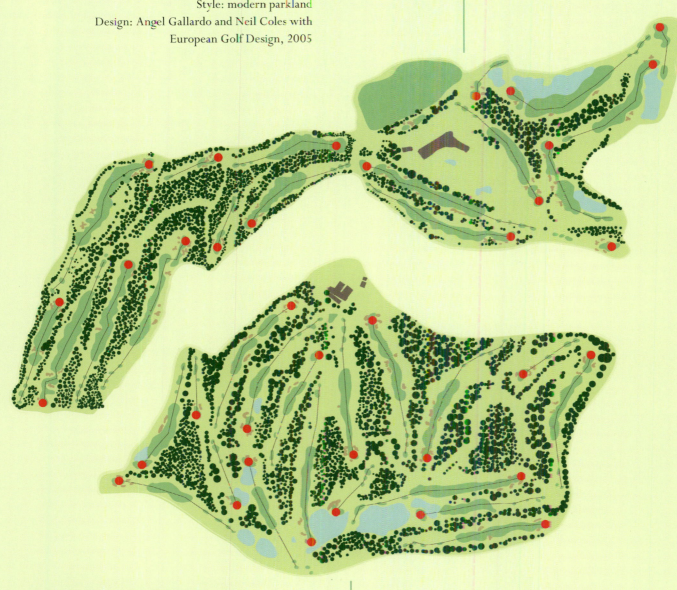

PGA Catalunya Stadium Course

18 holes, 6,809 yards, par 72
Handicap: male 28, female 36
Style: modern parkland
Design: Angel Gallardo and Neil Coles
with European Golf Design, 1998

Le Méridien Penina Golf & Resort

Penina, Portugal

Sir Henry Cotton was both a hard worker and a bon vivant. He would practice until his hands bled, and then he would step into his Rolls-Royce. "The best is always good enough for me," was the philosophy of this two-time British Open winner. He later made a name for himself as a golf course architect, building the first course on the Algarve and laying the foundation for a boom like none other—now more than 30 courses are lined up cheek by jowl in Southern Portugal. Penina Championship was the first, opened in 1966. The course is not particularly long, but longer hitters always tend to slip up because of the water hazards. The resort's hotel does not attempt to take center stage with exalted luxury, because the shining star is the historic championship course itself. Two additional 9-hole courses at the resort offer even beginners an exciting place to play.

Sir Henry Cotton war harter Arbeiter und Lebemann zugleich. Er trainierte, bis ihm die Hände bluteten, doch anschließend stieg er in seinen Rolls-Royce. „Das Beste ist immer gut genug für mich", lautete das Credo des zweimaligen British Open-Gewinners. Später machte er sich als Golfplatzarchitekt einen Namen, baute den ersten Platz an der Algarve und legte den Grundstein für einen Boom sondergleichen – mittlerweile reihen sich mehr als 30 Courses im Süden Portugals aneinander. Penina Championship ist das Original, 1966 eröffnet. Der Platz ist nicht sonderlich lang, aber Wasserhindernisse verbauen sorglosen Longhittern immer wieder den Weg. Das dazugehörige Hotel drängt sich nicht mit exaltiertem Luxus in den Vordergrund, denn der Star ist hier der historische Championship-Platz – und zwei weitere 9-Loch-Plätze im Resort bieten auch Anfängern ein spannendes Betätigungsfeld.

Sir Henry Cotton était aussi travailleur qu'il était épicurien. Il s'entrainait jusqu'à ce que ses mains fussent en sang. Puis il partait au volant de sa Rolls-Royce. « Je me contente toujours de ce qu'il y a de meilleur » était le credo du double vainqueur du British Open. Plus tard, il s'est fait un nom en tant qu'architecte de parcours de golf en modelant son premier terrain dans l'Algarve, prémices d'un boom sans pareil – une série de 30 parcours ont suivi dans le sud du Portugal. Penina Championship, l'original, a été inauguré en 1966. Le parcours n'est pas particulièrement long, mais les obstacles d'eau se trouvent toujours sur le chemin des frappeurs impétueux. L'hôtel dont il dépend ne mise pas sur un luxe exalté, car ici, la vedette, c'est le parcours historique : le Championship et les deux 9-trous supplémentaires du complexe qui offrent également aux débutants un terrain de jeu exigeant.

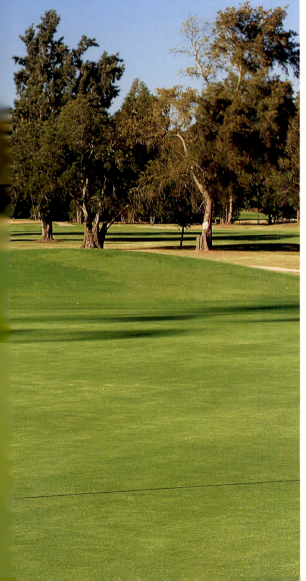

Le Méridien Penina Golf & Resort

Portimão, 8501-952 Penina
Portugal
T +35 128 2420 200, reservations.penina@lemeridien.com
www.lemeridien.com/penina

Rooms: 188 rooms and suites.

Facilities: kids club, pool, gym, tennis courts, 5 restaurants, 4 bars, golf, tennis courts, archery, beach club, jogging trail.

Services: 24 h front desk, car rental, laundry, doctor on call.

Located: 40 miles (65 kilometers) from Faro Airport.

Penina Championship Course

18 holes, 6,869 yards, par 73
Handicap: male 28, female 36
Style: parkland
Design: Sir Henry Cotton, 1966

Vale do Lobo

Algarve, Portugal

Those who travel to the Algarve and stand at hole 16 of the Royal Course can truly grasp what it's all about here, despite the luxurious atmosphere: It's about golf in its most elemental form. With an almost 655-foot-long par 3, players tee off over red cliffs and through spray from the Atlantic while taking the constant wind into account. It's like Scotland or Ireland, only much warmer. That's why hole 16 on the Royal Golf Course may well be the most photographed hole in Europe, though the Ocean Course is also very photogenic, particularly on the back nine holes. Vale do Lobo is the experience of a lifetime, a huge resort devoted to fulfilling every need, 365 days a year—from its own shopping center to 15 restaurants and different types of sports to the Beach Club. The clubhouse has the most lavish sandwiches to be found in the Algarve—multi-story creations that are almost too impressive to eat.

Wer an die Algarve reist und an der 16 des Royal Course steht, begreift, worum es hier trotz der luxuriösen Atmosphäre geht: um Golf in seiner ursprünglichsten Form. Beim fast 200 Meter langen Par 3 muss über rote Klippen und atlantische Gischt abgeschlagen werden, außerdem gilt es, den steten Wind mit einzuberechnen. Das ist wie Schottland oder Irland – bloß in deutlich wärmeren Temperaturen. Die 16 dürfte daher das meistabgelichtete Golfloch Europas sein, doch auch der Ocean Course erweist sich als fotogen, vor allem auf den hinteren neun Bahnen. Vale do Lobo ist ein Fest fürs Leben, ein riesiges Resort, das 365 Tage im Jahr keine Wünsche offen lässt, vom eigenen Shopping-Center über 15 Restaurants und verschiedensten Sportarten bis zum Beach Club. Im Clubhaus gibt es übrigens die üppigsten Sandwiches der Algarve – mehrstöckige Ungetüme, die zum Essen fast zu schade sind.

Quiconque se retrouvant dans l'Algarve au départ du numéro 16 du Royal Course comprend l'essence du lieu malgré le luxe environnant : le golf, au sens original du terme. Pour ce par 3 long de 200 mètres, il s'agit de frapper au-dessus des écueils rouges et contre les embruns de l'Atlantique tout en tenant compte du vent incessant. On se croirait en l'Écosse ou en Irlande, mais avec des températures sensiblement plus élevées. Le trou numéro 16 pourrait d'ailleurs bien être le plus photographié d'Europe, même si l'Ocean Course se révèle aussi particulièrement photogénique. Vale do Lobo est une ode à la vie, un vaste complexe qui sait combler tous les désirs 365 jours par an avec sa propre galerie commerciale, ses quinze restaurants, ses sports à la carte ou son Beach Club. Au clubhouse se trouvent les sandwiches les plus copieux de l'Algarve – des monstres de plusieurs étages que l'on dévore non sans scrupules.

Vale do Lobo

Almancil, 8135-864 Algarve
Portugal
T +35 128 9353 000, vdl@vdl.pt
www.valedolobo.com

Rooms: apartments, townhouses, and villas.

Facilities: 15 restaurants, bars, pools, beach, children's FunZone, spa.

Services: 24 h front desk, car rental, security service, medical center, free parking, internal circuit bus.

Located: 30 minutes from Faro Airport.

Royal Golf Course

18 holes, 6,626 yards, par 72
Handicap: male 28, female 36
Style: tree-lined and open parkland with cliff top
Design: Sir Henry Cotton in 1968, with later changes in 1997
by Rocky Rocquemore

Ocean Golf Course

18 holes, 6,711 yards, par 72
Handicap: male 28, female 36
Style: sea view parkland
Design: Sir Henry Cotton in 1968,
with later changes in 2003 by Rocky Rocquemore

Emirates Palace

Abu Dhabi, United Arab Emirates

Of all the luxury hotels in the world, the Emirates Palace in Abu Dhabi sets the standards. The construction costs of the oriental palace totaled three billion US dollars—it holds the record as the most expensive hotel project in the world. Every guest has a private butler as well as 14 restaurants to choose from. A staff of 1,500 takes care of about 400 rooms. This fairytale world offers state-of-the-art comfort, a private beach over a half mile long, and the Anantara Spa with hammam. Carved out of the desert at great expense, the nearby Abu Dhabi Golf Club is flawlessly maintained and features what is probably the most unusual clubhouse in the world—designed to look like a falcon with outstretched wings. Training champions can practice their swing on the largest driving range in the Gulf region, while beginners can hone their skills on the adjacent 9-hole course.

Unter allen Luxushotels dieser Welt setzt das Emirates Palace in Abu Dhabi Maßstäbe. Die Baukosten des orientalischen Palastes beliefen sich auf drei Milliarden US-Dollar – damit hält es den Rekord als teuerster Hotelbau der Welt. Jeder Gast hat seinen privaten Butler und kann unter 14 Restaurants wählen; insgesamt sind 1 500 Angestellte für die rund 400 Zimmer zuständig. Die Märchenwelt verfügt über modernsten Komfort, einen kilometerlangen Privatstrand und das Anantara Spa mit Hamam. Der nahe Abu Dhabi Golf Club ist mit viel Aufwand der Wüste abgetrotzt, besticht durch seine perfekte Pflege – und bietet das wohl ungewöhnlichste Clubhaus der Welt in Form eines Falken mit gespreizten Flügeln. Trainingsweltmeister können auf der größten Driving Range der Golfregion an ihrem Schwung arbeiten, Anfänger feilen auf dem angrenzenden 9-Loch-Platz an ihrem Spiel.

Parmi tous les hôtels de luxe de ce monde, l'Emirates Palace d'Abu Dhabi est une référence. La construction de ce palais d'Orient a coûté trois milliards de dollars, un record mondial actuel pour un hôtel. Chaque client dispose de son domestique attitré et peut choisir parmi quatorze restaurants ; au total, 1 500 personnes travaillent dans cet hôtel de quelque 400 chambres. Ce monde merveilleux propose un confort ultramoderne, un kilomètre de plage privée et un spa avec hammam : le Anantara. L'Abu Dhabi Golf Club tout proche, qui a surgi du désert au prix d'efforts colossaux, séduit par son entretien irréprochable. Il dispose du clubhouse le plus inhabituel du monde avec sa forme évoquant celle d'un faucon aux ailes déployées. Les champions peuvent travailler leur swing sur le plus grand practice du golfe Persique, alors que les débutants préféreront faire leurs armes sur le 9-trous attenant.

Emirates Palace

West Corniche Road, 39999 Abu Dhabi
United Arab Emirates
T +971 269 090 00, info.emiratespalace@emiratespalace.ae
www.kempinski.com/abudhabi

Rooms: 394 rooms and suites.
Facilities: 14 restaurants, 2 bars, nightclub/lounge, 2 pools, 2 gyms.
Services: 24 h room service, boat rental.
Located: 30 minutes from Abu Dhabi Airport, 120 minutes from Dubai Airport.

Emirates Golf Club

Emirates Hills 2, Dubai
United Arab Emirates
www.emiratesgolf.com

Dubai Creek Golf Club

Baniyas Road, Dubai
United Arab Emirates
www.dubaigolf.com/dubai-creek-golf-yacht-club.aspx

General golf reservations: T +971 438 012 34
golfbooking@dubaigolf.com
www.dubaigolf.com

Dubai Creek Course

18 holes, 6,857 yards, par 71
Handicap: male 28, female 36
Style: parkland along creek
Redesign: Thomas Björn, 2005

The Faldo Course

18 holes, 7,348 yards, par 73
Handicap: male 28, female 45
Style: natural valley parkland
Redesign: Nick Faldo, 2005

The Majlis Course

18 holes, 7,301 yards, par 72
Handicap: male 28, female 45
Style: desert parkland
Design: Karl Litten, 1988

La Résidence des Cascades

Soma Bay, Egypt

The view is most beautiful from the top, which is why this resort is perched on the highest point of Soma Bay. The Egyptian peninsula on the Red Sea was skillfully developed for the luxury segment. One of six impressive hotels in this area, La Résidence promotes ecotourism and received an award for its efforts in 2010. The spa specializes in seawater treatments and is an international leader in thalasso therapy. It also features unusual treatments such as underwater massages. The golf course, designed by Gary Player, winds around the hotel complex and cleverly integrates links and desert features—ranging from areas subject to constant wind to typically sandy, austere desert. Immediately adjacent to the course, beginners can practice on a 9-hole course, also designed by the wiry South African. In addition, Soma Bay is a popular diving destination: A 1,300-foot jetty leads divers directly to the house reef.

Von oben ist der Blick am schönsten, und deswegen thront das Resort auf dem höchsten Punkt von Soma Bay. Die ägyptische Halbinsel am Roten Meer wurde geschickt für das Luxussegment erschlossen; La Résidence ist hier eines von sechs beeindruckenden Hotels, das sich um umweltverträglichen Tourismus bemüht und dafür 2010 mit einer Auszeichnung belohnt wurde. Das Spa hat sich auf Meeresbehandlungen spezialisiert und ist in der Thalassotherapie weltweit führend. Auch Besonderheiten wie Unterwasser-Massagen werden angeboten. Der Gary-Player-Platz windet sich direkt um den Hotelkomplex und vereint auf einzigartige Weise Links- und Wüstenfeatures, vom steten Wind bis zu den typischen sandigen Waste-Areas. Direkt nebenan können Anfänger auf einem 9-Loch-Platz üben, der ebenfalls von dem drahtigen Südafrikaner gebaut wurde. Soma Bay ist außerdem ein beliebtes Tauchziel: Ein 420 Meter langer Holzsteg führt mitten hinein ins Hausriff.

En général, la vue est plus belle d'en haut. C'est la raison pour laquelle le complexe trône sur la baie de Soma et la mer Rouge. La Résidence, qui a été récompensée en 2010 pour son engagement dans un tourisme respectueux de l'environnement, se trouve avec cinq autres hôtels d'exception sur une presqu'île égyptienne exclusivement dédiée au luxe. Le spa, centre de thalassothérapie réputé dans le monde entier, propose des soins spéciaux comme les massages en immersion. Le golf signé Gary Player cerne le complexe hôtelier en associant au désert les caractéristiques d'un parcours links, comme en témoigne le vent incessant et les « waste areas » de sable. Les débutants s'exerceront sur le 9-trous attenant, lui aussi réalisé par le Sud-Africain. Par ailleurs, la baie de Soma est une destination prisée pour la plongée : le complexe dispose d'un ponton en bois de 420 mètres qui mène les plongeurs directement au milieu du récif.

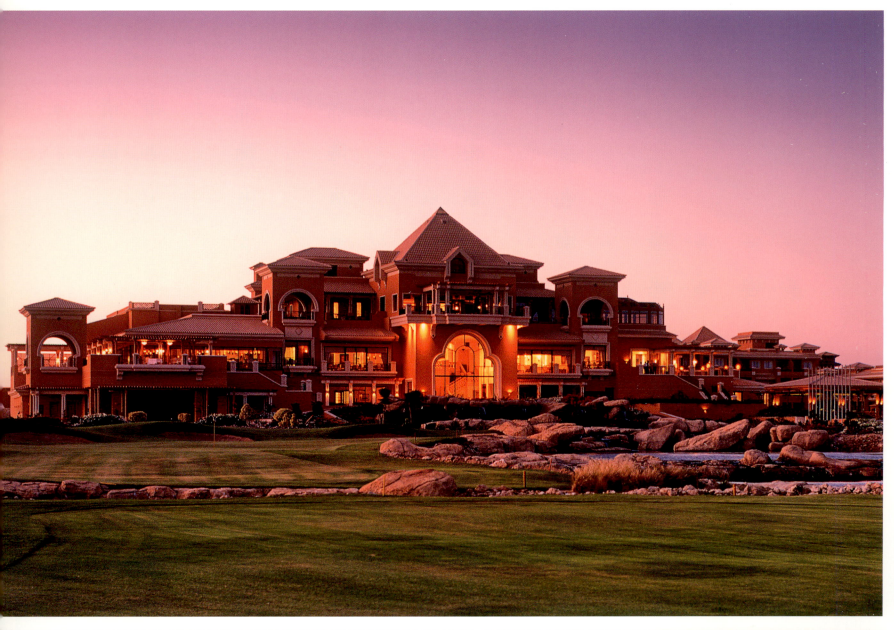

84   La Résidence des Cascades *Soma Bay, Egypt*

La Résidence des Cascades

48 Km Safaga Road, Soma Bay
Egypt
T +20 653 562 600
www.residencedescascades.com
Rooms: 210 rooms and 39 suites.
Facilities: 2 restaurants, 4 bars and lounges, spa, gym, watersports, tennis, golf, kids club, parking lot.
Services: 24 h front desk, beach shuttle, medical care, car rental.
Located: 28 miles (45 kilometers) from Hurghada Airport, located on the highest point of Soma Bay area.

The Cascades Championship Golf Course

18 holes, 6,991 yards, par 72
Handicap: 36
Style: desert links course with extensive water hazards
Design: Gary Player, 1999

Amanjena

Marrakech, Morocco

A Moroccan fairy-tale castle near Marrakech, flanked by palms and olive trees: Amanjena means "peaceful paradise," and every guest feels like a sultan in these imaginative surroundings. Amelkis, the open and hilly 27-hole golf course, adjoins the resort, while the second nine holes incorporate more water hazards. Steeped in tradition, the Royal Golf Course is just a few minutes away. Perhaps most impressive is Amanjena's location at the foot of the High Atlas Mountains—a majestic, snow-capped range that rises to more than 13,000 feet. The hotel offers guided tours into the mountains: on foot, by bicycle, or in a comfortable car. Some of the best places to relax in the resort include the well-stocked two-story international library with fireplace, the oriental spa with two hammams, and the 108-foot heated outdoor swimming pool surrounded by hibiscus bushes.

Eine marokkanische Märchenburg nahe Marrakesch, gesäumt von Palmen und Olivenbäumen: Amanjena heißt „friedliches Paradies", und in dieser fantasievollen Umgebung fühlt sich jeder Gast wie ein Sultan. Der 27-Loch-Platz Amelkis grenzt direkt an das Resort und präsentiert sich offen und hügelig, während auf den zweiten neun Löchern nach und nach mehr Wasser ins Spiel kommt. Der traditionsreiche Royal Golf Course liegt nur wenige Minuten entfernt. Vor allem aber beeindruckt die Lage Amanjenas am Fuß des Atlasgebirges, das sich majestätisch und schneebedeckt auf über 4 000 Meter erhebt. Das Hotel bietet auch geführte Touren in die Berge an – zu Fuß, per Fahrrad oder ganz bequem im Auto. Beste Orte der Entspannung im Resort sind die doppelstöckige, gut bestückte internationale Bibliothek mit Kamin, das orientalische Spa mit zwei Hamams und der 33 Meter lange, beheizte Außenpool, umrahmt von Hibiskussträuchern.

Une citadelle fabuleuse près de Marrakech, bordée de palmiers et d'oliviers : à Amanjena, qui signifie « paradis paisible », chaque client se sent comme un sultan au milieu de cet environnement merveilleux. Le parcours Amelkis de 27-trous qui voisine avec le complexe est ouvert et vallonné alors que sur le 9-trous, chacun fait la part toujours plus belle à l'eau. Le Royal Golf Course, empreint de tradition, est à quelques minutes à peine de l'impressionnant site d'Amanjena qui se trouve au pied de l'Atlas et dont les majestueux sommets enneigés culminent à plus de 4 000 mètres. L'hôtel propose d'ailleurs des sorties guidées dans la montagne – à pied, en vélo ou, plus confortablement, en voiture. Les secrets de la détente du complexe : les deux étages de la bibliothèque internationale et sa cheminée, le spa oriental avec ses deux hammams et la piscine extérieure chauffée de 33 mètres entourée d'hibiscus.

Amanjena

Route de Ouarzazate, Km 12, 40000 Marrakech
Morocco
T +212 524 399 000, amanjena@amanresorts.com
www.amanjena.com

Rooms: 32 pavillons, 6 two-bedroom maisons, and one big "Al-Hamra" maison.
Facilities: restaurant, bar, library, boutique, spa, pool, tennis, golf, parking lot, private gardens.
Services: 24 h front desk, bicycle rental, airport transfer.
Located: 20 minutes from Marrakech-Menara Airport.

Amelkis Golf Club

Route de Ouarzazate, Km 12, 40000 Marrakech
Morocco
T +212 444 044 14

The Amelkis Golf Course

18 holes (a further 9-hole course has been added), 7,250 yards, par 72
Handicap: 54
Style: nature parkland
Design: Cabell B. Robinson, 1995

Constance Belle Mare Plage

Poste de Flacq, Mauritius

Paradise has 36 holes: The Belle Mare Plage Resort on Mauritius is spread out along a sandy beach over a mile long that looks exactly the way you might imagine a vacation getaway in your dreams: palm trees for shade, the ocean shimmering a perfect blue-green, and snow-white sand glittering in the sun. The Legend and Links golf courses are located directly at the resort and extend over 345 acres. Hole 17 on the slightly older Legend course is unforgettable: a not overly long par 3 with plenty of ocean between the tee and green. On the Links course, added later, hole 6 is particularly memorable: a formidable par 5 whose green is protected by volcanic rock. At the resort, guests can choose between seven restaurants and six bars—and the Lobster Nights at the Indigo Beach Club should not be missed. The spa rounds out its offerings with yoga and meditation classes.

Das Paradies hat 36 Löcher: Das Belle Mare Plage Resort auf Mauritius zieht sich an einem zwei Kilometer langen Sandstrand entlang, der exakt so aussieht, wie man es sich in seinen Urlaub-für-immer-Träumen vorstellt: Palmen spenden Schatten, das Meer schimmert grünblau, der Sand strahlt schneeweiß. Die beiden Golfplätze Legend und Links direkt am Resort breiten sich auf 140 Hektar aus. Unvergesslich ist die Bahn 17 auf dem etwas älteren Legend-Platz, ein nicht allzu langes Par 3 mit viel Ozean zwischen Tee und Grün. Auf dem später hinzugefügten Links-Platz bleibt vor allem die 6 in Erinnerung, ein gewaltiges Par 5, dessen Grün von Vulkangestein verteidigt wird. Im Resort haben Gäste die Wahl zwischen sieben Restaurants und sechs Bars. Nicht entgehen lassen sollten sie sich die „Lobster Nights" im Indigo Beach Club. Das Spa bietet außerdem Yoga- und Meditationskurse an.

Le paradis a 36 trous : le Belle Mare Plage sur l'île Maurice s'étend le long d'une plage de deux kilomètres. Il correspond parfaitement à l'image que l'on se fait des destinations de rêves : le sable blanc comme la neige, l'ombre des palmiers et le scintillement de la mer turquoise… Les deux terrains de golf Legend et Links s'étalent sur 140 hectares directement à côté du complexe. Le numéro 17 du parcours le plus ancien, le Legend, est inoubliable : un par 3, pas si long, mais où l'océan sépare le tee du green. Sur le terrain Links, aménagé dans la foulée, le 6 marque les esprits : un puissant par 5 au green protégé par de la roche volcanique. Dans le complexe, les clients ont le choix parmi sept restaurants et six bars. Il ne faut manquer sous aucun prétexte les « Lobster nights » à l'Indigo Beach Club. Par ailleurs, le spa propose des séances de yoga et de méditation.

Constance Belle Mare Plage

Poste de Flacq
Mauritius
T +230 4022 600, info@bellemareplagehotel.com
www.bellemareplagehotel.com
Rooms: 235 rooms and suites, 20 villas, 1 Presidential Villa.
Facilities: 7 restaurants, 6 bars and lounges, kids club, spa, gym, tennis, golf, mini golf, water sports.
Services: 24 h front desk and room service, car rental, medical treatment.
Located: 31 miles (50 kilometers) from Sir Seewoosagur Ramgoolam International Airport of Mauritius.

The Links Course

18 holes, 6,501 yards, par 71
Handicap: male 28, female 36
Style: traditional links with rolling fairways
Design: Rodney Wright, Peter Allis, 2002

The Legend Course

18 holes, 6,584 yards, par 72
Handicap: male 28, female 36
Style: traditional links with rolling fairways
Design: Hugh Baiocchi, 1994

Heritage Awali Golf & Spa Resort

Bel Ombre, Mauritius

The resort's beach is much too nice to simply spend your time sunbathing. Dinghies, surfboards, and kayaks stand at the ready, and if guests prefer something faster, they can go waterskiing. Regardless of their handicap, golfers will enjoy playing on the resort's spacious 18-hole course. Hole 14 is impressive: a par 5 with a double dogleg where players need to take water into account along its entire length. Those new to the sport are free to experiment with their swing on the meticulously groomed 9-hole course. Evenings are for entertainment: After dinner at Infinity Blue, a restaurant on the beach, or at the French-inspired Château de Bel Ombre, native dance groups perform the famous sega, a style of music and dance that was once meant to drive out the devil, but has long since become an exciting experience for the senses.

Der Strand des Resorts ist viel zu schade, um sich einfach nur zu bräunen. Dingis, Surfbretter und Kajaks liegen bereit, und wen es nach noch mehr Geschwindigkeit verlangt, der fährt Wasserski. Auf dem großzügig angelegten 18-Loch-Platz des Resorts haben Spieler jeder Handicap-Klasse ihren Spaß. Beeindruckend ist die 14, ein Par 5 mit doppeltem Dogleg, an dem im gesamten Verlauf Wasser ins Spiel kommt. Wer gerade erst mit dem Sport begonnen hat, kann auf dem makellos gepflegten 9-Loch-Platz ungestört an seinem Schwung herumexperimentieren. Der Abend gehört der Unterhaltung: Nach einem Dinner im Strandrestaurant Infinity Blue oder im französisch inspirierten Château de Bel Ombre führen einheimische Tanzgruppen den berühmten Sega auf, einen Musik- und Tanzstil, der einst den Teufel austreiben sollte, längst aber zu einem sinnlichen und aufregenden Erlebnis geworden ist.

Il serait dommage de se contenter de séances de bronzage sur la plage de ce complexe : canots, surfs et kayaks sont à la disposition des clients, et les amateurs de vitesse peuvent réserver des séances de ski nautique. Le vaste golf 18-trous du complexe comblera tous les joueurs, quel que soit leur handicap. Le numéro 14 est impressionnant ; l'eau est omniprésente tout au long de ce par 5 en double dog-leg. Pour les débutants, le 9-trous impeccablement entretenu laisse tout le temps nécessaire à l'étude de leur swing. La soirée est un moment privilégié pour profiter des divertissements : après un dîner au restaurant de plage Infinity Blue ou à celui du Château de Bel Ombre d'inspiration française, des groupes locaux exécutent le célèbre Sega. Il s'agit d'une musique et d'un style de danse qui autrefois servaient à exorciser le démon et qui sont devenus aujourd'hui une stimulante expérience des sens.

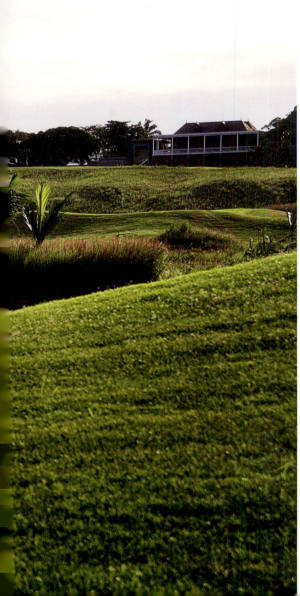

Heritage Awali Golf & Spa Resort

Domaine de Bel Ombre, Bel Ombre
Mauritius
T +230 6011 500 , info@heritageawali.mu
www.heritageawali.mu/index.php
Rooms: 154 rooms, 5 suites, and 1 villa.
Facilities: 4 restaurants, 2 bars, 3 pools, gym, spa, water sports, golf, tennis.
Services: 24 h front desk, evening entertainment.
Located: 1 hour from Sir Seewoosagur Ramgoolam International Airport of Mauritius.

Heritage Golf Club Golf Course

18 holes, 7,116 yards, par 72
Handicap: 36
Style: parkland between mountain and sea
Design: Peter Matkovich, 1994

Constance Lémuria Resort

Praslin, Seychelles

On the sandy beaches of Anse Kerlan in the Seychelles, nature is so untouched that endangered sea turtles can still lay their eggs in the sand here. The Lémuria Resort on the island of Praslin fits in harmoniously with the untouched flora and fauna. With a typical island design, the lodges have interiors that feature tropical wood, marble, and granite, and are minimalistic yet luxurious at the same time. All suites have views of the Indian Ocean. The three restaurants serve regional cuisine in all its diversity. The par-70 course is a watery affair, and the last six holes are hilly, which means that players are guaranteed magnificent views of the unspoiled countryside. The dramatically beautiful 18th hole, a tricky par 5 with water along the entire right side, requires a confident drive to bring home a good score or a match play victory.

Die Natur ist am Seychellen-Strand Anse Kerlan noch so intakt, dass die vom Aussterben bedrohten Wasserschildkröten hier ihre Eier im Sand ablegen können. Das Lémuria Resort auf der Insel Praslin fügt sich harmonisch in die unberührte Flora und Fauna ein – die inseltypischen Lodges mit ihrem Interieur aus Tropenholz, Marmor und Granit sind minimalistisch und luxuriös zugleich gehalten. Alle Suiten blicken auf den Indischen Ozean. In den drei Restaurants wird landestypische Küche in all ihrer Vielfalt präsentiert. Der Par-70-Platz ist eine wässrige Angelegenheit, und die letzten sechs Bahnen fallen hügelig aus, was prächtige Blicke über die unverdorbene Landschaft garantiert. Vor allem an der dramatisch schönen 18, einem kniffligen Par-5-Loch mit Wasser auf der gesamten rechten Seite, ist ein sicherer Drive notwendig, um den Score oder den Matchplay-Sieg sicher ins Clubhaus zu bringen.

Aux Seychelles, la plage de Anse Kerlan a si bien su préserver son espace naturel que des tortues menacées d'extinction viennent toujours y pondre leurs œufs dans le sable. Le complexe Lémuria, sur l'île Praslin, s'intègre harmonieusement dans cet environnement intact : les lodges typiques de l'île sont aménagés de manière minimaliste et luxueuse avec un intérieur associant marbre, granit et bois tropicaux ; toutes les suites ont vue sur l'océan Indien. Les trois restaurants proposent de la cuisine autochtone dans toute sa diversité. Tout est question d'eau dans ce parcours par 70. De plus, les six derniers trous présentent de beaux dénivelés, ce qui garantit une vue magnifique sur ces paysages vierges. En particulier, le somptueux et épineux numéro 18 est un par 5 qui longe l'eau sur toute la longueur du côté droit et requiert un drive des plus sûrs pour confirmer son score ou rentrer victorieux au clubhouse.

Constance Lémuria Resort

Anse Kerlan, Praslin
Seychelles
T +248 4281 281, info@lemuriaresort.com
www.lemuriaresort.com
Rooms: 96 suites, 8 villas with pool, 1 Presidential Villa.
Facilities: 3 restaurants, 4 bars, spa, pool, gym, tennis, water sports, kids club, library, boutique.
Services: limousine and helicopter transfers from and to airport, bicycle rental,
arrival/departure lounge with bathrooms, car rental, doctor on call.
Located: 5 minutes from Praslin Airport.

The Lémuria Golf Championship Golf Course

18 holes, 6,138 yards, par 70
Handicap: 36
Style: coves, woods, and parkland
Design: Rodney Wright, helped by the champion Marc-Antoine Farry, 2000

The Palace of the Lost City

Sun City Resort, South Africa

The 338-room complex with its fantastical African architecture is among the most unusual buildings in the world. Sun City is a gigantic leisure park with casinos and safari trails; it took shape on the drawing board and is considered to be the Las Vegas of Africa. It is no coincidence that it also shares the nickname of Las Vegas: Sin City. Covering over 212 square miles of untouched (and malaria-free) landscape, South African golf legend Gary Player created two outstanding 18-hole courses that host important professional tournaments every year—including the Million Dollar Challenge where the victor can look forward to a seven-digit check. The Lost City Course in particular requires steady nerves from amateur players: Crocodiles lurk in the water hazard on hole 13. Regular guests of the resort include Elton John, Julio Iglesias, and Tina Turner.

Der 338-Zimmer-Komplex gehört mit seiner afrikanischen Fantasiearchitektur zu den ungewöhnlichsten Bauwerken der Welt. Die Stadt Sun City, ein gigantischer Freizeitpark mit Casinos und Safari-Trails, entstand auf dem Reißbrett und gilt als Las Vegas Afrikas. Nicht umsonst teilt sie auch den Spitznamen „Sin City", Stadt der Sünde. In 55 000 Hektar unberührter (und malariafreier) Landschaft schuf die südafrikanische Golflegende Gary Player zwei herausragende 18-Loch-Plätze, auf denen jedes Jahr bedeutende Profi-Turniere stattfinden, so etwa die Million Dollar Challenge, bei der sich der Sieger über einen siebenstelligen Scheck freuen darf. Vor allem der Lost City Course verlangt dem Hobbygolfer einiges an Nerven ab: Im Wasserhindernis an Bahn 13 tummeln sich Krokodile. Zu den Stammgästen des Resorts gehören unter anderem Elton John, Julio Iglesias und Tina Turner.

L'architecture africaine-fantastique place ce complexe de 338 chambres parmi les constructions les plus atypiques du monde. La ville de Sun City qui passe aujourd'hui pour le Las Vegas africain est un gigantesque parc d'attractions avec casinos et piste de safari né de l'imagination de ses créateurs. Son surnom, « Sin City » ou la ville des péchés, n'est pas innocent. Au cœur de 55 000 hectares de nature préservée (mais sans risque de malaria), la légende du golf sud-africain Gary Player a créé deux 18-trous exceptionnels qui accueillent chaque année d'importants tournois professionnels, comme le Million Dollar Challenge, dont le vainqueur remporte un chèque à sept chiffres. L'un parcours, le Lost City, a la particularité de jouer avec les nerfs des golfeurs amateurs : l'obstacle d'eau du 13 est envahi de crocodiles. Le complexe compte notamment parmi ses visiteurs de marque Elton John, Julio Iglesias et Tina Turner.

The Palace of the Lost City

0316 Sun City Resort
South Africa
T +27 117 807 878 , ceurope@za.suninternational.com
www.suninternational.com
Rooms: 338 rooms and suites.
Facilities: restaurants, bars, pool, conference rooms, kids club, spa, sauna, squash, tennis, entertainment center with shops and casino.
Services: 24 h front desk, children's program, safaris, Segway and bike rental.
Located: 103 miles (165 kilometers) from Johannesburg O.R. Tambo airport.

The Lost City Golf Course

18 holes, 6,983 yards, par 72
Handicap: not specific
Style: desert parkland
Design: Gary Player, 1993

The Gary Player Golf Course

18 holes, 8,000 yards, par 72
Handicap: male 28, female 36
Style: modern parkland
Design: Gary Player, 1979

Fancourt

George, South Africa

Fancourt has a distinctly more European atmosphere than competing Sun City. The architecture is elegantly minimalistic instead of African fantasy, and that is due in large part to Hasso Plattner, the German owner. And yet Africa is more present here than elsewhere. In the Garden Route, visitors can look forward to encounters with the fascinating "big five" of wildlife: lions, leopards, buffalo, rhinos, and elephants. The "big three," on the other hand, refer to the resort's golf courses: The Links, Montagu, and Outeniqua. The Links is one of the best courses in Africa. To achieve this masterpiece, Gary Player and his design team spent months traveling through Scotland and Ireland to draw inspiration from the fairways and greens so steeped in history. The 2003 Presidents Cup was held on The Links course, which ended in a historic tie after a playoff between Ernie Els and Tiger Woods.

In Fancourt gibt man sich deutlich europäischer als die Konkurrenz in Sun City. Die Architektur ist edel reduziert statt afrikanisch-märchenhaft, was möglicherweise am deutschen Besitzer Hasso Plattner liegt. Dabei ist Afrika hier präsenter als anderswo. In der Garden Route können Besucher auf Begegnungen mit den faszinierenden „Big Five" hoffen: Löwe, Leopard, Büffel, Nashorn und Elefant. Die „Big Three" dagegen sind die Golfplätze des Resorts: The Links, Montagu und Outeniqua. The Links gehört zu den besten Plätzen in Afrika. Gary Player und sein Design-Büro reisten für ihr Meisterwerk monatelang durch Schottland und Irland, um sich von den geschichtsträchtigen Fairways und Grüns inspirieren zu lassen. Auf dem Links Course fand 2003 der Presidents Cup statt, der nach einem Play-off zwischen Ernie Els und Tiger Woods mit einem historischen Unentschieden endete.

Le Fancourt affiche un caractère nettement plus européen que la concurrence de Sun City. L'architecture est élégante et minimaliste plutôt qu'africaine-fantastique. Peut-être faut-il y voir le choix du propriétaire allemand Hasso Plattner. Pourtant, l'Afrique y est omniprésente. Sur la Garden Route, les visiteurs peuvent espérer croiser les fascinants « Big Five » : le lion, le léopard, le buffle, le rhinocéros et l'éléphant. Les « Big Three » pour leur part, sont les golfs du complexe : le Links, le Montagu et l'Outeniqua. Le Links compte parmi les plus beaux terrains en Afrique. Gary Player et son équipe ont voyagé des mois entiers en Écosse et en Irlande pour s'inspirer de fairways et de greens chargés d'histoire afin de concevoir leur chef-d'œuvre. En 2003, le play-off de la President Cup, qui a eu lieu sur le parcours Links, s'est soldé par un match nul historique entre Ernie Els et Tiger Woods.

Fancourt

Montagu Street, 6529 George
South Africa
T +27 448 040 010, reservations@fancourt.co.za
www.fancourt.co.za

Rooms: 115 rooms, including suites at Fancourt Hotel, 18 luxury suites at Manor House.
Facilities: 4 restaurants, bars, parking lot, pool, spa, gym, tennis, golf, kids club.
Services: 24 h front desk, excursions.
Located: 4 miles (7 kilometers) from George Airport, 261 miles (420 kilometers) from Cape Town.

Outeniqua

18 holes, 6,944 yards, par 72
Handicap: male 24, female 36
Style: parkland
Design: Gary Player, 1990

The Links

18 holes, 7,565 yards, par 73
Handicap: male 24, female 36
Style: dune-style landscape and modern parkland
Design: Gary Player, 2000

Montagu

18 holes, 7,385 yards, par 72
Handicap: male 24, female 36
Style: parkland
Design: Gary Player, 1990

Pezula Resort Hotel & Spa

Knysna Lagoon, South Africa

This location is an experience, even for seasoned travelers. The resort on a cliff near the Knysna Lagoon is bordered on one side by the magnificent lagoon and on the other by the Indian Ocean. The advantage of this site continues on the golf course: Water is everywhere, and the views are intoxicating. Yet the course demands full concentration from the very first hole, a 546-yard par 5, while 16 and 17 are short but tricky par-4 holes. With its opulent spa, the hotel is situated in the heart of the Garden Route, one of the most popular travel destinations in Africa. In addition to tennis, squash, horseback riding, and guided hikes through untouched forests, guests can also try their hand at cricket, a sport unfamiliar to most. For those who are in a hurry: Two Lear jets are at the disposal of well-to-do guests—unfortunately, the jets are not included in the room rate.

Diese Lage ist selbst für Vielgereiste ein Erlebnis. Das Resort auf einem Felsen an der Knysna-Lagune ist auf der einen Seite von der großartigen Lagunen-landschaft umgeben, auf der anderen Seite vom Indischen Ozean. Dieser Standortvorteil setzt sich auf dem Golfplatz fort: Wasser ist allgegenwärtig, die Ausblicke sind berauschend. Dabei erfordert der Course volle Konzentration schon ab Bahn 1, einem 500 Meter langen Par 5, oder auf den kurzen, aber trickreichen Par-4-Bahnen 16 und 17. Dazu liegt das Hotel mit seinem opulenten Spa auch noch mitten auf der Garden Route, einem der populärsten Reiseziele Afrikas. Neben Tennis, Squash, Ausritten und geführten Wandertouren durch unberührte Waldlandschaften kann man sich auch in dem für die meisten eher ungewohnten Sport Cricket versuchen. Wer es ganz eilig hat: Betuchten Gästen stehen zwei Learjets zur Verfügung – die leider nicht im Zimmerpreis enthalten sind.

Même les plus grands voyageurs sont unanimes : le site est unique. Perché sur un rocher, le complexe est cerné d'un côté par la somptueuse lagune de Knysna et de l'autre côté par l'océan Indien. Le golf est tout aussi exceptionnel. L'eau y est omniprésente et la vue enivrante. Pourtant, il requiert une concentration absolue dès le premier trou, un long par 5 de 500 mètres, mais aussi sur les trous 16 et 17, deux courts par 4 très techniques. L'hôtel se trouve sur la Garden Route, une destination qui compte parmi les plus prisées d'Afrique. Outre un luxueux spa, l'hôtel dispose d'installations permettant la pratique du tennis, du squash et de l'équitation. Il propose également des randonnées guidées au milieu de forêts préservées et permet de s'initier à un sport méconnu en Occident : le cricket. Autre service, malheureusement non inclus dans le prix de la chambre : deux jets privés sont à la disposition des clients les plus pressés.

Pezula Resort Hotel & Spa

Lagoonview Drive, 6570 Knysna
South Africa
T +27 443 023 333, info@pezula.com
www.pezula.com
Rooms: 78 Luxury and Superior Suites, 5 Private Residence Villas.
Facilities: Zachary's gourmet restaurant, Café Z, bar, cigar lounge, library, spa, gym, golf, kids club, designer boutique, business center.
Services: 24 h front desk, shuttle service to beach, horse riding.
Located: 1 hour from George International Airport.

Pezula Golf Club

Lagoonview Drive, 6571 Knysna
South Africa
T +27 443 025 310, golf@pezulagolf.com
www.pezulagolf.com

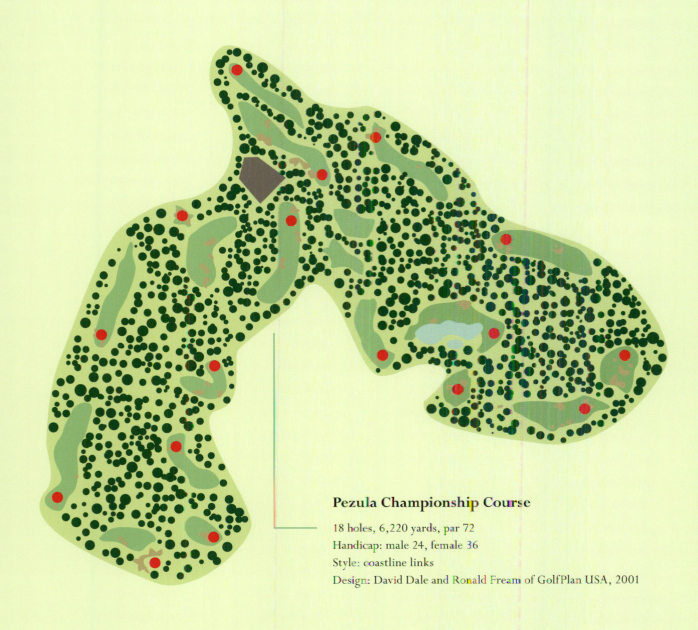

Pezula Championship Course

18 holes, 6,220 yards, par 72
Handicap: male 24, female 36
Style: coastline links
Design: David Dale and Ronald Fream of GolfPlan USA, 2001

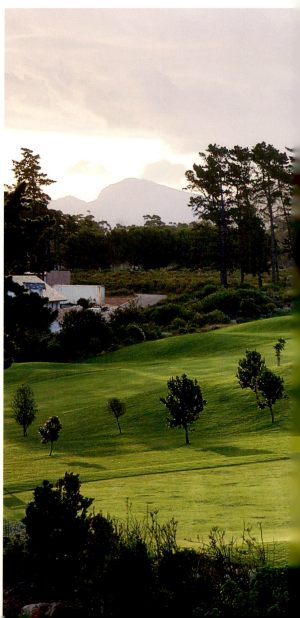

Arabella Hotel & Spa

Kleinmond, South Africa

In the heart of the Kogelberg Nature Reserve and surrounded by highly diverse flora, the Arabella Group has created a sanctuary on 276 acres just an hour away from Cape Town. The spa in particular enjoys an international reputation. The two-hour Rainforest Experience is a multi-faceted and relaxing water and steam treatment. Guests who tend to prefer more uncomplicated luxuries can retreat to the Cigar Lounge. The golf course traverses the rich landscape and extends along the Bot River lagoon. The fairways and greens are meticulously maintained, although the players rarely look down—the panorama is far too breathtaking. Ronan Keating and Samuel L. Jackson enjoy making the circuit here. Players who would like to firm up their drives while on vacation are in good hands with Alison Sheard, one of the best golf professionals to ever come out of South Africa.

Mitten im Kogelberg-Reservat und umgeben von artenreicher Flora hat die Arabella-Gruppe auf 112 Hektar einen idyllischen Zufluchtsort geschaffen, nur eine Stunde außerhalb von Kapstadt. Vor allem das Spa genießt Weltruf. Die zweistündige „Rainforest Experience" ist eine entspannende Wasser- und Wasserdampfbehandlung. Gäste, die eher zum bedenkenlosen Genießen neigen, lassen in der Cigar Lounge die Seele baumeln. Der Golfplatz zieht sich durch die artenreiche Landschaft und an der riesigen Lagune des Bot River entlang. Der Pflegezustand der Fairways und Grüns ist exzellent, auch wenn die Blicke der Spieler selten nach unten gerichtet sind – zu grandios ist das Panorama. Ronan Keating und Samuel L. Jackson drehen hier gern ihre Runden. Wer im Urlaub seinen Schwung stabilisieren will, ist bei der Proette Alison Sheard bestens aufgehoben, einer der besten Golferinnen, die Südafrika je hervorgebracht hat.

Au cœur de la réserve Kogelberg et dans un environnement floral d'une grande diversité, le groupe Arabella a créé, à une heure de voiture de la ville du Cap, un refuge de 112 hectares. Le lieu doit avant tout sa réputation internationale à son spa. La « Rainforest Experience » est une séance de relaxation de deux heures qui utilise autant l'eau que la vapeur. Les clients les plus sybarites préfèreront se retirer dans le Cigar Lounge. Le parcours s'étend quant à lui le long de la vaste lagune de la rivière Bot au milieu d'une nature d'une grande richesse. L'entretien apporté aux fairways et aux greens est irréprochable, mais rares sont les joueurs qui baissent leur regard pour le remarquer — pour cause, le panorama est grandiose. Ronan Keating et Samuel L. Jackson y ont leurs habitudes. Les joueurs voulant profiter du séjour pour stabiliser leur swing peuvent s'en remettre à Alison Sheard, une des meilleures golfeuses que l'Afrique du Sud ait vues naître.

Arabella Hotel & Spa

R44 to Kleinmond, 7195 Kleinmond
South Africa
T +27 282 840 000, reservations@arabellahotelandspa.com
www.africanpridehotels.com/arabella-hotel-spa.html
Rooms: 145 rooms and suites.
Facilities: garden, parking lot, restaurants, bars, spa, indoor and outdoor pools, golf, tennis.
Services: 24 h front desk, valet service, babysitting.
Located: 56 miles (90 kilometers) from Cape Town International Airport.

Arabella Golf Course

18 holes, 7,019 yards, par 72
Handicap: not specific
Style: parkland on the banks of Bot River lagoon
Design: Peter Matkovich, 1999

The Fairmont Banff Springs

Banff Springs, Alberta, Canada

The construction of The Fairmont Banff Springs in 1888 was what truly launched tourism in the Rocky Mountains. It is not just the hotel's location in the heart of Canada's Banff National Park (a UNESCO World Heritage Site) that makes it truly unique; modeled after a Scottish castle, the hotel formidably combines the best of two worlds. In the winter, The Fairmont Banff Springs is a ski resort, while in the summer it transforms into a golf resort with a 27-hole course set amid majestic mountain scenery. Yet even in the winter, avid golfers can practice inside in comfort in a high-quality simulator. When the huge structure stood empty for years in the 1960s, it inspired Stephen King to write his horror classic "The Shining." With its Willow Stream spa, the hotel is now more splendid than ever before—in deep snow or summer sunshine alike.

Der Bau des Hotels im Jahr 1888 gab die Initialzündung für den Tourismus in den Rocky Mountains. Es ist nicht nur die Lage im kanadischen Banff-Nationalpark (einem UNESCO-Welterbe), die das Haus, das einem schottischen Schloss nachempfunden ist, einzigartig macht, sondern auch die formidable Kombination des Besten aus zwei Welten. Im Winter fungiert das Banff Springs Hotel als Skiresort, im Sommer wandelt es sich zum Golfresort mit 27-Loch-Platz in majestätischer Bergwelt. Wer auch im Winter nicht vom Golfen lassen will, kann an einem hochwertigen Simulator im warmen Inneren üben. Als das riesige Haus in den 60er Jahren lange Zeit leer stand, inspirierte das Stephen King zu seinem Horrorroman „Shining", doch inzwischen funkelt das Hotel mit seinem Willow Stream Spa prächtiger denn je – ob im Tiefschnee oder der Sommersonne.

La construction de cet hôtel, en 1888, est à l'origine du tourisme dans les montagnes Rocheuses. L'établissement, construit sur le modèle d'un château écossais, est unique – non seulement par sa situation au cœur du parc national Banff (inscrit au patrimoine mondial de l'UNESCO), mais aussi car il réunit deux mondes opposés : son emplacement est idéal pour les sports d'hiver et l'été, il se mue en un complexe de golf de choix grâce à son parcours 27-trous au milieu des montagnes majestueuses. En période hivernale, les golfeurs ne voulant rien perdre de leur swing pourront s'entraîner bien au chaud sur un simulateur frappant de réalisme. Dans les années 1960, l'immense bâtiment, alors à l'abandon, inspira Stephen King pour l'écriture de son roman « Shining ». Aujourd'hui, quelle que soit la saison, la splendeur de l'hôtel est plus éclatante que jamais, notamment grâce à son spa : le Willow Stream.

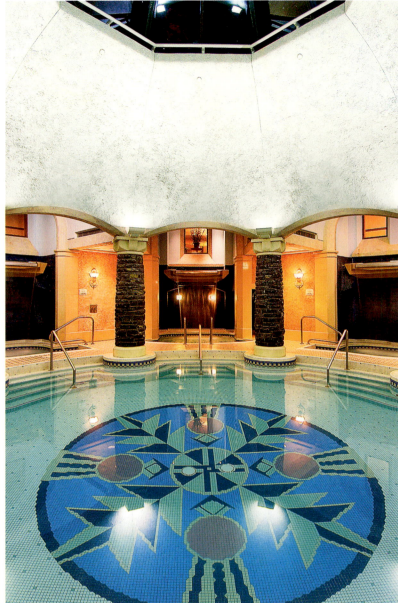

The Fairmont Banff Springs

405 Spray Avenue, T1L1J4 Banff, Alberta
Canada
T +1 403 7622 211, banffsprings@fairmont.com
www.fairmont.de/banffsprings

Rooms: 770 rooms and suites.

Facilities: 5 restaurants, 2 bars, spa, gym, indoor and outdoor pool, business center, parking lot.

Services: 24 h front desk, babysitting, ski shuttle, medical care, car rental.

Located: 1.45 hours from Calgary International Airport, located on the banks of the scenic Bow River, a 10-minute walk from downtown Banff.

The Fairmont Banff Springs Golf Course
Stanley Thompson (Rundle/Sulphur)

27 holes in total
Stanley Thompson (Rundle/Sulphur): 18 holes, 6,938 yards, par 71
Tunnel Mountain Course (not shown on map): 9 holes, 3,357 yards, par 36
Handicap: not specific
Style: natural parkland in the heart of Canada's Rocky Mountains
Design: 18 holes, Stanley Thompson, 1928, 9 holes were added by
Cornish and Robinson in 1989

The Breakers Palm Beach

Palm Beach, Florida, USA

An American classic: The resort in Palm Beach with its two towers is nearly an icon of tourism in the United States. The first wealthy hotel guests began traveling to Florida in 1896—and paid four dollars per night. The estate burned down twice in its history, and in 1926 it was rebuilt in its current incarnation. 73 artisans were brought over from Italy to work on the magnificent ceiling paintings. The two championship courses are available exclusively to hotel guests. The Ocean Course was constructed at the same time as the first hotel and is the oldest 18-hole course in Florida. The Breakers Course, on the other hand, was created in 1968 and was completely reconstructed by Rees Jones in 2004. The Beach Club not only features a private beach, but also five swimming pools, four whirlpool spas, and nine restaurants—living the good life on an ultra-grand scale.

Hier handelt es sich um einen amerikanischen Klassiker: Das Resort in Palm Beach ist mit seinen beiden Türmen beinahe eine Ikone des US-Tourismus. Schon 1896 kamen die ersten begüterten Hotelgäste nach Florida – und zahlten vier Dollar pro Nacht. Zweimal brannte das Anwesen vollständig nieder; 1926 entstand es in seiner heutigen Form neu. Für die gewaltigen Deckengemälde wurden 73 Spezialisten aus Italien einbestellt. Die beiden Championship-Plätze stehen den Hotelgästen und Club-Mitgliedern exklusiv zur Verfügung. Der Ocean Course entstand zeitgleich mit dem ersten Hotelbau und ist der älteste 18-Loch-Platz in Florida, während der 1968 geschaffene Breakers Course im Jahr 2004 von Rees Jones gründlich überarbeitet wurde. Der Beach Club verfügt nicht nur über einen Privatstrand, sondern gleich über fünf Swimmingpools, vier Whirlpools und neun Restaurants – das gute Leben im XXL-Format.

Il s'agit ici d'un classique aux États-Unis : les deux tours du complexe de Palm Beach sont une icône du tourisme américain. Déjà en 1896, les premiers riches clients se rendaient en Floride et devaient débourser quatre dollars pour y passer la nuit. La propriété a connu deux graves incendies ; l'édifice dans son état actuel date de 1926. À l'époque, les fresques monumentales des plafonds ont requis l'intervention de 73 spécialistes italiens. Les deux terrains de championnat sont exclusivement réservés à la clientèle de l'hôtel. L'Ocean Course, créé lors de la construction initiale de l'hôtel, est le plus ancien 18-trous de Floride, alors que le Breakers Course a été entièrement refait en 2004 par Rees Jones. Le Beach Club propose non seulement une plage privée, mais aussi cinq piscines, quatre jacuzzis et neuf restaurants : la belle vie, version XXL.

The Breakers Palm Beach

One South County Road, Palm Beach, FL 33480
USA
T +1 561 6556 611
www.thebreakers.com

Rooms: 540 rooms, including 68 suites.
Facilities: Oceanfront Spa, tennis, 9 restaurants, 5 pools, 4 whirlpool spas,
25 luxury beach bungalows, watersports, private beach, fitness centers, 11 shops, family entertainment center.
Services: 24 h front desk.
Located: 8 miles (13 kilometers) from Palm Beach International Airport.

The Breakers Rees Jones Course

1550 Flagler Parkway, West Palm Beach, FL 33411
USA
T +1 561 6536 320
www.thebreakers.com

The Breakers Rees Jones Course

18 holes, 7,100 yards, par 72
Handicap: not specific
Style: parkland
Design: remodeled by Rees Jones, 2004

The Breakers Ocean Golf Course

18 holes, 6,100 yards, par 70
Handicap: not specific
Style: ocean side parkland
Design: 1896 by Alexander H. Findlay,
redesigned by Brian Silva, 2000

The Biltmore Hotel

Coral Gables, Florida, USA

Recently overhauled to the tune of 100 million dollars, the Biltmore is once again as beautiful as it was when it opened in 1926 and became the symbol of the Jazz Age—the Golden Twenties, when the Great Depression and World War II were still far away. Johnny Weissmuller, later to play Tarzan in the movies, worked as a swimming instructor at the pool, and Franklin D. Roosevelt and Al Capone were guests in the suites. Legendary stars such as Walter Hagen and Gene Sarazen as well as baseball legend Babe Ruth played on the golf course. Today, the Biltmore is an established part of the Miami social life. VIPs from throughout Florida drop by for the champagne brunch on Sundays. On the course, the final holes are something special: Hole 17 is a par 5 whose green is located on a peninsula, while hole 18 (par 4) has a dogleg to the left—players who like to slice the ball will have trouble arriving back at the clubhouse with a good score.

Gerade für 100 Millionen Dollar generalüberholt, strahlt das Biltmore wieder so schön wie zu seiner Eröffnung 1926, als der fantasievolle Bau zum Symbol des „Jazz Age" wurde – der Zeit der Goldenen Zwanziger Jahre, als Wirtschaftskrise und Weltkrieg noch fern waren. Der spätere Tarzan Johnny Weissmüller arbeitete am Pool als Schwimmlehrer, in den Suiten wohnten Franklin D. Roosevelt und Al Capone. Auf dem Golfplatz spielten Altstars wie Walter Hagen und Gene Sarazen sowie Baseball-Legende Babe Ruth. Noch heute ist das Biltmore ein Fixpunkt des gesellschaftlichen Lebens in Miami; zum sonntäglichen Champagner-Brunch finden sich VIPs aus ganz Florida ein. Auf dem Platz haben es besonders die Schlusslöcher in sich: Die 17 ist ein Par 5, dessen Grün auf einer Halbinsel liegt, die 18 (Par 4) biegt als Dogleg nach links ab – wer den Ball gern mit Slice spielt, wird Schwierigkeiten haben, mit einem guten Score ins Clubhaus zu kommen.

Après complète rénovation et 100 millions de dollars dépensés, le Biltmore resplendit comme lors de son ouverture en 1926, quand son exubérance symbolisait le « Jazz Age », pendant les années folles, alors que la crise économique et la Seconde Guerre mondiale étaient encore loin. Le futur Tarzan, Johnny Weissmüller, était le maître nageur de la piscine, tandis que les suites étaient occupées par Franklin D. Roosevelt et Al Capone. Le golf accueillait des célébrités comme Walter Hagen, Gene Sarazen ou la légende du base-ball Babe Ruth. Aujourd'hui, la haute société de Miami se réunit toujours au Biltmore ; les brunchs dominicaux rassemblent les VIP de toute la Floride autour de coupes de champagne. Le parcours a ses particularités, surtout les derniers trous : le 17 est un par 5 dont le green se trouve sur une presqu'île, alors que le 18 (par 4) est un dog-leg à gauche – les adeptes du slice auront d'ailleurs des difficultés à rentrer au clubhouse avec un beau score.

The Biltmore Hotel

1200 Anastasia Avenue, Coral Gables, FL 33134
USA
T +1 877 7234 044, reservations@biltmorehotel.com
www.biltmorehotel.com
Rooms: 273 rooms, including 130 suites.
Facilities: spa, 3 signature restaurants, pool, golf, tennis, gym, children's activities.
Services: 24 h front desk, concierge service, wedding service, event catering.
Located: 6 miles (10 kilometers) from Miami International Airport.

The Biltmore Golf Course

18 holes, 6,800 yards, par 71
Handicap: not specific
Style: nature parkland
Design: Donald Ross, 1925, restoration by Brian Silva, 2007

Turnberry Isle Miami

Miami, Florida, USA

Big is beautiful in the recently renovated 400-room Mediterranean-style hotel. Turnberry Isle to the north of Miami Beach promises a top-notch active vacation getaway with two 18-hole courses, designed by US Open Champion Ray Floyd and completely reconstructed for $45 million; a state-of-the-art spa and fitness center; four tennis courts; and a private beach club on the Atlantic. At Bourbon Steak, the hotel's restaurant, steaks from prime organic beef are skillfully prepared on wood-fired grills. Children in particular are sure to enjoy the three pools, thanks in no small part to the 180-foot water slide that is over 32 feet high. Guests who prefer to find their adrenaline fix on the golf course should book the Miller Course. Hole 14 is not only 590 yards long, but players almost always face into the wind. The 18th hole on the Soffer Course features the largest artificial waterfall in Florida.

Big is beautiful in dem 400-Zimmer-Hotel im mediterranen Stil, das komplett neu restauriert wurde. Zwei 18-Loch-Plätze im Norden von Miami Beach, von US-Open-Champion Ray Floyd entworfen und für 45 Millionen Dollar komplett überarbeitet, ein Fitnessstudio auf allerneuestem Stand, vier Tennisplätze, ein privater Beach Club am Atlantik – Turnberry Isle verspricht Aktivurlaub auf höchstem Niveau, selbst kulinarisch: Im Hotelrestaurant Bourbon Steak werden die Steaks aus bestem Bio-Fleisch schonend auf Holzkohlegrills zubereitet. An den drei Pools haben vor allem Kinder ihre Freude, nicht zuletzt dank einer 55 Meter langen und zehn Meter hohen Wasserrutsche. Wer das Adrenalin lieber auf den Golfplätzen sucht, sollte den Miller Course buchen. Bahn 14 ist nicht nur 540 Meter lang, sondern spielt sich auch noch fast immer in den Wind hinein. Dafür bietet der Soffer Course an Bahn 18 den größten künstlichen Wasserfall Floridas.

L'immensité fait la beauté de cet hôtel de 400 chambres au décor méditerranéen entièrement restauré. Au nord de Miami Beach, deux 18-trous signés Ray Floyd, ancien vainqueur de l'US Open, ont été entièrement rénovés pour 45 millions de dollars, et sont assortis d'une salle de gym moderne, de quatre courts de tennis, d'un club de plage sur l'Atlantique : le séjour promet d'être sportif. Sur le plan culinaire, le restaurant Bourbon Steak propose des steaks bio de qualité exceptionnelle grillés au feu de bois. Trois piscines feront la joie des enfants : un toboggan de 55 mètres culmine notamment à dix mètres de hauteur. Les visiteurs qui recherchent plutôt l'adrénaline sur un golf doivent réserver le parcours Miller. Ils apprécieront le numéro 14, non seulement pour ses 540 mètres, mais aussi pour le vent qui se mêle au jeu presque systématiquement. Le parcours Soffer n'est pas en reste avec le 18 sur lequel se dresse la plus haute cascade artificielle de Floride.

Turnberry Isle Miami

19999 W Country Drive Aventura, Miami, FL 33180
USA

T +1 866 6127 739, tir.reservations@turnberryislemiami.com
www.turnberryislemiami.com

Rooms: 392 rooms and suites.
Facilities: 3 restaurants, bar, lounge, business center, beach club, spa, gym, 3 pools, golf, tennis, ATM.
Services: 24 h front desk and room service, concierge, parking, children's program, babysitting.
Located: 30 minutes from Miami International Airport and 20 minutes from Fort Lauderdale-Hollywood International Airport.

Soffer Course

18 holes, 7,047 yards, par 71
Handicap: not specific
Style: modern parkland
Design: Robert Trent Jones, Sr., 1971
Redesign: Raymond Floyd, 2006

Miller Course

18 holes, 6,417 yards, par 70
Handicap: not specific
Style: modern parkland
Design: Robert Trent Jones, Sr., 1971
Redesign: Raymond Floyd, 2007

Four Seasons Resort Scottsdale at Troon North

Scottsdale, Arizona, USA

Located at the foot of Pinnacle Peak in the high Sonoran desert, one of the largest desert landscapes in the world, this resort offers Southwestern style architecture and individual adobe casitas. Guests have two golf courses to choose from: The Pinnacle, designed by Tom Weiskopf in 1996, and The Monument, also conceived by the former British Open Champion. Both are very special courses that simply cannot be found in Europe. Verdant green fairways wend through an austere landscape, where cacti tower along the edges of the fairways and players even encounter the occasional roadrunner. Guests who would like to see even more of the surroundings (the Sonoran desert is highly diverse), can take part in guided hikes and bicycle tours along old Indian trails, or they can explore even more remote landscapes by jeep.

Im Hochland der Sonora-Wüste, in einer der größten Wüstenlandschaften der Welt, bietet das Resort Architektur im Southwestern-Stil und individuelle Apartmentbauten für die Gäste, direkt unterhalb des alles dominierenden Gipfels Pinnacle Peak. Zwei Golfplätze stehen den Gästen zur Verfügung: The Pinnacle wurde 1996 von Tom Weiskopf gebaut, und für The Monument zeichnet ebenfalls der ehemalige British-Open-Champion verantwortlich. Beides sind ganz besondere Plätze, die es so in Europa einfach nicht gibt – saftig-grüne Fairways ziehen sich durch eine karge Landschaft, Kakteen ragen am Fairwayrand empor, und manchmal grüßt ein Wegekuckuck, auch im Deutschen besser bekannt als Roadrunner. Wer noch mehr von der Natur sehen will (Sonora gilt als sehr artenreiche Wüste), kann sich bei geführten Wander- und Radtouren auf alte Indianerpfade begeben oder mit dem Jeep in noch entlegenere Landschaften vordringen.

Sur les plateaux du désert de Sonora, l'un des plus vastes paysages désertiques du monde, le complexe propose à ses hôtes des appartements individuels dans le plus pur style du sud-ouest, directement au pied du Pinnacle Peak qui domine la vallée. Deux terrains sont proposés : The Pinnacle, créé en 1996, et The Monument, tous deux conçus par Tom Weiskopf, l'ancien vainqueur du British Open. Ces deux parcours présentent des particularités simplement introuvables en Europe : les fairways verdoyants bordés de cactées s'étendent sur un paysage aride et reçoivent parfois la visite d'un grand géocoucou, mieux connu sous le nom de « Bip Bip ». Les amoureux d'espaces vierges (Sonora est un désert célèbre pour sa biodiversité) apprécieront les balades guidées à pied, à vélo ou en véhicules tout terrain sur les anciens sentiers des Indiens, au milieu de sites encore plus isolés.

Four Seasons Resort Scottsdale at Troon North

10600 E Crescent Moon Drive, Scottsdale, AZ 85262
USA
T +1 480 5155 700
www.fourseasons.com/scottsdale
Rooms: 210 rooms, including 22 suites.
Facilities: pool, golf, gym, tennis, spa, restaurants.
Services: 24 h front desk, children's amenities, business service.
Located: 10 miles (16 kilometers) from Scottsdale Municipal Airport.

Troon North Golf Club

10320 E Dynamite Boulevard, Scottsdale, AZ 85262
USA
T +1 480 5855 300
www.troonnorthgolf.com

The Monument Course

18 holes, 7,070 yards, par 72
Handicap: not specific
Style: desert parkland
Design: Jay Morrish and Tom Weiskopf, 1990

The Pinnacle Course

18 holes, 7,025 yards, par 72
Handicap: not specific
Style: parkland through natural ravines and foothills
Design: Tom Weiskopf, 1995, opened 1996, renovated 2007

Hyatt Regency Scottsdale

Scottsdale, Arizona, USA

Scottsdale is the golfing capital of the United States. Outstanding courses and perfect weather conditions twelve months a year draw an increasing number of tour players from around the world and convince them to put down roots in Arizona—Geoff Ogilvy and Aaron Baddeley from Australia and Paul Casey from England are just a few examples. Golf tourists can enjoy Scottsdale to the full as well. The Hyatt Regency nestles between palms and cacti at the foot of the McDowell range, a sacred location for the Yavapai Indians. This luxury resort offers three 9-hole loops, each with completely different features. The Lakes has a wide variety of water features—which comes as no surprise. The Dunes is reminiscent of Scottish links courses, and Arroyo has wide and generous fairways that meander picturesquely through the desert landscape. How about a ride out into the desert after a round of golf? An experienced guide is at your service.

Scottsdale ist die Golfhauptstadt der Vereinigten Staaten. Herausragende Plätze und zwölf Monate im Jahr perfekte Wetterbedingungen sorgen dafür, dass sich immer mehr Tour-Spieler aus aller Welt in Arizona niederlassen, etwa die Australier Geoff Ogilvy und Aaron Baddeley sowie der Engländer Paul Casey. Auch Golf-reisende können Scottsdale in vollen Zügen genießen. Das Hyatt Regency liegt zwischen Palmen und Kakteen unterhalb der McDowell-Bergkette, dem heiligen Ort der Yavapai-Indianer. Das Luxusresort bietet drei 9-Loch-Schleifen mit ganz unterschiedlichen Charakteristika. Auf dem Lakes Course kommt – keine Überraschung – viel Wasser ins Spiel, The Dunes erinnert an schottische Links-Plätze, und Arroyo zieht sich malerisch mit großzügig breiten Fairways durch die Wüstenlandschaft. Wie wäre es nach der Runde mit einem Ausritt in die Wüste? Ein erfahrener Guide steht dafür zur Verfügung.

Scottsdale est la capitale américaine du golf. Les parcours exceptionnels et les conditions climatiques idéales tout au long de l'année poussent toujours plus de joueurs professionnels du monde entier à s'installer en Arizona, à l'instar des Australiens Geoff Ogilvy et Aaron Baddeley ou de l'Anglais Paul Casey. Les golfeurs de passage peuvent également profiter pleinement de Scottsdale. Le Hyatt Regency a été construit au pied de la chaîne de montagnes McDowell, lieu sacré pour les Indiens Yavapai. Ce complexe de luxe propose, entre palmiers et cactus, trois parcours 9-trous aux caractéristiques differentes. The Lakes fait largement appel – sans surprise – à l'eau. The Dunes est un clin d'œil aux parcours links écossais et l'Arroyo déroule ses larges fairways sur un paysage désertique époustouflant. Et si vous êtes tenté par une sortie à cheval dans le désert à la fin d'une partie, un guide expérimenté est à disposition.

Hyatt Regency Scottsdale

7500 E Doubletree Ranch Road, Scottsdale, AZ 85258
USA
T +1 480 4441 234, resscott@hyatt.com
www.scottsdale.hyatt.com
Rooms: 493 rooms, including 31 suites.
Facilities: restaurants, bars, conference rooms, car rental desk, pools, spa, golf, tennis.
Services: 24 h in-room dining, babysitting.
Located: 16 miles (25 kilometers) from Sky Harbor International Airport.

Gainey Ranch Golf Club

7600 E Gainey Club Drive, Scottsdale, AZ 85258-1600
USA
T +1 480 9510 022
www.gaineyranchcc.com

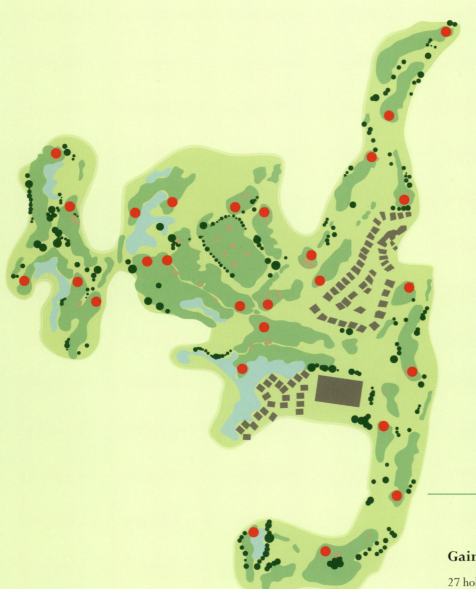

Gainey Ranch Golf Club

27 holes, 3 courses (Lakes, Dunes, Arroyo),
par 36 (for each of the 9-hole courses)
Handicap: not specific
Style: garden-like parkland surrounded by desert
Design: Benz and Poellot
Arroyo – Lakes Course: 18 holes, 6,800 yards, par 72
Lakes – Dunes Course: 18 holes, 6,614 yards, par 72
Dunes – Arroyo Course: 18 holes, 6,662 yards, par 72

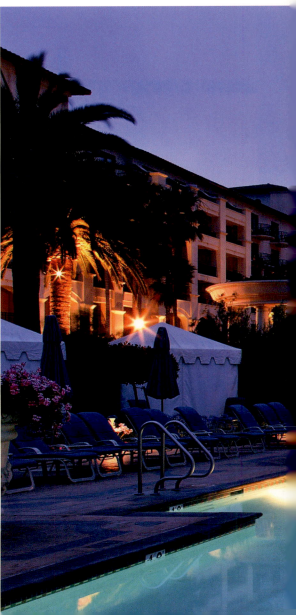

St. Regis Monarch Beach

Dana Point, California, USA

Tuscan style in California, the Pacific at your feet, and a Robert Trent Jones course outside your door: This American interpretation of the dolce vita is particularly successful between Los Angeles and San Diego. At Stonehill Tavern, created by celebrated designer Tony Chi, guests can choose from 500 bottles of top California wines from Sonoma and Napa. Spa Gaucin, on the other hand, features Mediterranean specialties, including a full body massage using Chardonnay oil. The golf course is one of the very few in California located directly on the coast. Hole 3, a short par 4, completely borders the Pacific. And players who would like to test the length of their drives can look forward to hole 7—a 612-yard par 5 monster with a double fairway. Those who still haven't had enough of the water can take in the sunset while enjoying a plate of fresh seafood and listening to the surf at the Monarch Bay Club.

Toskana-Stil in Kalifornien, den Pazifik zu Füßen und einen Robert-Trent-Jones-Golfplatz vor der Tür: Die amerikanische Interpretation des Dolce Vita ist zwischen Los Angeles und San Diego besonders gut geglückt. In der Stonehill Tavern, entworfen von Stardesigner Tony Chi, können Gäste aus 500 Flaschen kalifornischer Spitzenweine aus Sonoma und Napa wählen. Das Spa Gaucin setzt dagegen auf mediterrane Spezialitäten, etwa die Ganzkörpermassage mit Chardonnay-Öl. Der Golfplatz gehört zu den ganz wenigen in Kalifornien, die direkt an die Küste grenzen. Bahn 3, ein kurzes Par 4, spielt sich komplett am Pazifik entlang; und wer seine Drivelänge testen will, ist an Bahn 7 gut aufgehoben, einem 560 Meter langen Par-5-Monster mit doppeltem Fairway. Wer vom Wasser noch nicht genug hat, genießt den Sonnenuntergang bei fangfrischen Meeresfrüchten auf dem Teller und der Brandung im Ohr im Monarch Bay Club.

La Toscane en Californie, l'azur du Pacifique et un parcours signé Robert Trent Jones en guise de jardin : la version américaine de la dolce vita située entre Los Angeles et San Diego est une véritable réussite. La taverne Stonehill, conçue par le grand designer Tony Chi, propose une sélection de 500 bouteilles des meilleurs vins californiens des vallées de Sonoma et Napa. Le Spa Gaucin mise quant à lui sur la tradition méditerranéenne, avec notamment un massage intégral à l'huile de chardonnay. Le golf compte parmi les rares parcours de Californie situés directement sur la côte. Le trou numéro 3, un court par 4, longe dans son intégralité le Pacifique. Les frappeurs voulant tester la portée de leur drive apprécient le 7, un monstrueux par 5 de 560 mètres de long avec double fairway. Les vrais amoureux de l'océan profitent du coucher de soleil en dégustant un plateau de fruits de mer au Monarch Bay Club avec en fond musical, le fracas des vagues.

St. Regis Monarch Beach

One Monarch Beach Resort, Dana Point, CA 92629
USA
T +1 949 2343 200
www.stregismb.com

Rooms: 400 rooms, including 75 suites.
Facilities: golf, spa, restaurants, lobby lounge, gym, beach, pools, tennis.
Services: 24 h room service, babysitting available.
Located: 25 minutes from Orange County/John Wayne Airport, 70 minutes from Los Angeles International Airport, and 73 minutes from
San Diego International Airport.

Monarch Beach Golf Links

33033 Niguel Rd Monarch Beach, CA 92629-4073
USA
T +1 949 2408 447
www.monarchbeachgolf.com

Monarch Beach Course

18 holes, 6,344 yards, par 70
Handicap: not specific
Style: sea view parkland
Design: Robert Trent Jones, Jr., 1983

One&Only Palmilla

San José del Cabo, Baja California, Mexico

Located on the southern tip of the Baja California peninsula, Los Cabos has become one of the most popular vacation spots in Mexico thanks in no small part to the One&Only resort which draws guests from the U.S. and Canada, particularly in the winter time. Jack Nicklaus is not only the best golfer of all time, here he has proven once again that he can also design fantastic courses. The 27-hole course of the Palmilla Club is divided into three loops—the Arroyo Nine, the Mountain Nine, and the Ocean Nine—and features cacti, dramatic elevation changes, four lakes, and breathtaking views of the Gulf of California. Hole 5 of the Mountain Nine is magnificent, a par 5 which courageous players can conquer with two drives—providing they decide to tackle the long drive over the water both times. Speaking of water, there's no need to pack a raincoat or umbrella—the region is one of the driest in the world.

Los Cabos an der Südspitze der Halbinsel Baja California hat sich zu einem der beliebtesten Urlaubsorte Mexikos entwickelt, nicht zuletzt dank des One&Only-Resorts, das vor allem zur Winterzeit Gäste aus dem Norden Amerikas anlockt. Jack Nicklaus ist nicht nur der beste Golfer aller Zeiten, sondern beweist hier einmal mehr, dass er auch fantastische Plätze entwerfen kann. Der 27-Loch-Course des Palmilla Clubs aus den drei Schleifen Arroyo Nine, Mountain Nine und Ocean Nine inmitten von Kakteen bietet beachtliche Höhenunterschiede, vier Seen und atemberaubende Blicke auf den Golf von Kalifornien. Grandios ist die 5 des Mountain Course, ein Par 5, das Mutige mit zwei Schlägen erreichen können – sofern sie beide Male den langen Schlag übers Wasser wagen. Apropos Feuchtigkeit: Regenkleidung und Schirm braucht sich niemand in das Bag zu stopfen, die Region gehört zu den niederschlagsärmsten der Welt.

Los Cabos, à la pointe sud de la péninsule de Baja California, est devenu l'un des lieux de villégiature préférés du Mexique. Le One&Only Palmilla y a certainement sa part de responsabilité, car il attire de nombreux clients nord-américains, surtout en hiver. Ici, Jack Nicklaus, non satisfait d'être l'un des meilleurs golfeurs de tous les temps, prouve une fois de plus qu'il peut créer de fantastiques terrains. Le parcours 27-trous du Palmilla Club, constitué des trois 9-trous Arroyo Nine, Mountain Nine et Ocean Nine propose, au milieu des cactées, d'impressionnants dénivelés, quatre lacs et des vues à couper le souffle sur le golf de Californie. Le numéro 5 de Mountain est un grandiose par 5 que les courageux peuvent réussir en deux coups – à condition de tenter deux fois une longue frappe au-dessus de l'eau. À propos d'humidité : les vêtements de pluie et le parapluie sont absolument superflus car la région compte parmi celles enregistrant les plus faibles précipitations au monde.

One&Only Palmilla

Km 7.5 Carretera Transpeninsular, CP 23400 San José Del Cabo
Mexico
T +52 624 1467 000, reservations@oneandonlypalmilla.com
palmilla.oneandonlyresorts.com
Rooms: 173 rooms with 12 categories.
Facilities: pool, golf, spa, restaurants, kids club.
Services: 24 h butler service.
Located: 13 miles (21 kilometers) from San José del Cabo Airport.

Palmilla Golf Club

Km 7.5 Carretera Transpeninsular, San José del Cabo
Mexico
T +52 621 445 250
www.palmillagc.com

Jack Nicklaus Signature Course

27 holes, 6,939 yards (Arroyo/Mountain), par 72
Handicap: male 28, female 36
Style: sea view parkland
Design: Jack Nicklaus, Arroyo Nine and Mountain Nine Course 1992, Ocean Nine Course 1997

Rosewood Mayakoba

Rivera Maya, Mexico

The geographic setting alone promises a carefree vacation. Situated on the Yucatán Peninsula between Cancún and Playa del Carmen and bordered by a sandy Caribbean beach on one side and tropical rainforest on the other, the hotel offers cool and minimalistic architectural design for a hot climate. Golfers are sure to enjoy playing the aptly named El Camaleón course, designed by two-time Majors Champion Greg Norman, as it meanders through jungle and mangrove stands before making its way along the coastline. Hole 15, for instance, is a short yet impressive par 3, with the turquoise-blue Caribbean shimmering on the slice side as a constant companion. In 2006 the course went down in history as the setting for the very first tournament of the PGA tour to take place outside of North America. The state-of-the-art Jim McLean Golf School promises longer and straighter drives.

Schon die geographische Lage verspricht sorglosen Urlaub. Auf der Yucatán-Halbinsel, zwischen Cancún und der Playa del Carmen, begrenzt von karibischem Sandstrand und tropischem Regenwald, bietet das Hotel kühl-reduzierte Architektur im heißen Klima. Für Golfer hat der zweifache Major-Champion Greg Norman einen angenehm zu spielenden Platz mit dem treffenden Namen El Camaleón entworfen, der sich mal durch den Dschungel und Mangroven windet und mal an der Küste entlang verläuft. An Bahn Nummer 15 etwa, einem kurzen und dennoch beeindruckenden Par 3, ist auf der Slice-Seite die türkisblau schimmernde Karibik ein ständiger Begleiter. Im Jahr 2006 schrieb der Platz Geschichte, denn auf ihm fand das erste Turnier der PGA Tour außerhalb Nordamerikas statt. Die erstklassig ausgestattete Golfschule von Jim McLean verspricht längere und geradere Schläge.

La situation géographique du complexe garantit un séjour des plus relaxants : sur la presqu'île du Yucatán, entre Cancún et Playa del Carmen, à la frontière entre les plages de sable des Caraïbes et la forêt tropicale, l'hôtel présente une architecture minimaliste dont la fraîcheur est bienvenue par grosse chaleur. Pour les golfeurs, Greg Norman, vainqueur de deux tournois majeurs, a créé un terrain très agréable à jouer, au nom seyant de El Camaleón, dû à sa situation côtière, lové entre jungle et mangrove. Sur le numéro 15 par exemple, un par 3 court mais spectaculaire, les reflets bleu-turquoise des Caraïbes accompagnent les joueurs sur tout le fairway. En 2006, le parcours est entré dans l'histoire du golf en accueillant le premier tournoi du circuit PGA organisé hors d'Amérique du Nord. L'école de golf de Jim McLean dispose de magnifiques installations et saura donc développer et affiner votre frappe.

Rosewood Mayakoba

Carretera Federal Cancún-Playa del Carmen Km 298, CP 77710 Solidaridad, Quintana Roo
Mexico
T +52 984 8758 000, mayakoba@rosewoodhotels.com
www.rosewoodhotels.com/en/mayakoba

Rooms: 128 suites.

Facilities: 3 restaurants, 2 bars, spa, yoga classes, infinity-edge and spa pools, water sports, kids club.

Services: 24 h front desk, concierge service, valet parking, butler service, 24 h in-room dining.

Located: 25 minutes from Cancun International Airport.

El Camaleón

18 holes, 7,024 yards, par 72
Handicap: male 28, female 36
Style: sea view parkland bending through tropical landscape
Design: Greg Norman, 2006

Four Seasons Resort Costa Rica

Peninsula Papagayo, Costa Rica

A peaceful country without a standing army, Costa Rica offers many natural wonders. Located on the Peninsula Papagayo on the country's northwest coast, Four Seasons Resort is committed not only to luxury but also to nature conservation. On over 62 miles of untouched beaches and in a strictly protected tropical dry forest, eco-adventurers can enjoy themselves in myriad eco-friendly ways—by taking kayak and catamaran tours, for instance, or exploring the lush flora and fauna of the forest from a network of sky walks—wooden suspension bridges that wind through the forest canopy. On the Arnold Palmer Golf Course, one of the best courses in Latin America, players can enjoy spectacular water views on 14 of the 18 holes. Hole 6, a par 4, is perhaps the most dramatic: From an elevated tee, players hit the ball onto a fairway located almost 200 feet downhill. The green is perched on a cliff above the Pacific.

Costa Rica ist ein friedlicher Staat, der keine stehende Armee unterhält und viele Naturwunder zu bieten hat. Auf der Halbinsel Papagayo im Nordwesten des Landes hat sich ein Resort angesiedelt, das sich nicht nur dem Luxus, sondern auch dem Naturschutz verschrieben hat. Auf fast 100 Kilometern unberührtem Strand und in streng geschütztem tropischem Trockenwald können sich Öko-Abenteurer auf die sanfte Art vergnügen, etwa bei Kajak- und Katamaran-Touren oder beim Skywalking über hölzerne Pfade, die sich auf Höhe der Baumwipfel mitten durch die üppige Flora und Fauna schlängeln. Auf dem Arnold-Palmer-Platz, einem der besten Courses Mittelamerikas, ist an 14 von 18 Bahnen Wasser mit von der Partie. Besonders eindrucksvoll präsentiert sich Loch 6, ein Par 4: Die Spieler schlagen von einer erhöhten Tee Box auf ein Fairway 60 Meter unter ihren Füßen. Das Grün liegt auf den Klippen über dem Pazifik.

Le Costa Rica est un pays paisible qui, au lieu d'entretenir une armée, ne demande qu'à partager ses nombreuses ressources naturelles. La presqu'île de Papagayo dans le nord-ouest du pays est le site choisi par le complexe qui mise non seulement sur le luxe, mais aussi sur la protection de la nature. Les éco-aventuriers au sens propre du terme trouveront leur bonheur avec près de 100 kilomètres de plage préservée et une forêt tropicale sèche très protégée, à découvrir en kayak, catamaran ou grâce à des parcours d'accrobranche qui se frayent un chemin au sommet des arbres, au milieu de la flore luxuriante et de la faune. Sur le golf Arnold-Palmer, un des meilleurs parcours d'Amérique centrale, les trous 14 à 18 intègrent l'eau dans le jeu. Le 6, un par 4, est le trou le plus impressionnant : les joueurs frappent depuis une aire de départ surplombant le fairway de 60 mètres. Le green se trouve sur une falaise qui domine le Pacifique.

Rooms: 120 rooms and 25 suites, 30 residences and villas with terraces, fully equipped kitchens, some of them with private plunge pools.
Facilities: 3 restaurants, bar and grill, 3 outdoor pools, 2 beaches, spa and fitness facilities, Championship golf course.
Services: 24 h in-room dining, hiking, sailing, snorkeling, kids and teens program.
Located: At the Gulf of Papagayo in the northwest of Costa Rica, a 40 minutes drive from the airport of Liberia.

Four Seasons Golf Club Costa Rica at Peninsula Papagayo

18 holes, 6,788 yards, par 72
Handicap: not specific
Style: ocean view parkland
Design: Arnold Palmer, 2004

Casa de Campo

La Romana, Dominican Republic

A Caribbean treasure island with 63 holes of golf—including the 18 amazing holes of Teeth of the Dog, one of the best courses in the world. "I created eleven holes and God created seven!" commented designer Pete Dye about his masterpiece on the ocean. With so much world-class golf, the resort in the Dominican Republic with its elegant, straightforward interior almost becomes secondary. The good life takes place in the outdoors. Casa de Campo is famous for its equestrian offerings: Dozens of horses fill the stables, eagerly waiting to head out on a trail ride. On three playing fields, even beginners can try their hand at the ancient and elite sport of polo. To wind up an eventful day, guests can relax on the hotel's own Minitas Beach over a legendary piña colada, served in a freshly picked pineapple.

Eine karibische Schatzinsel mit 63 Golflöchern, unter denen auch die 18 großartigen Bahnen von Teeth of the Dog zu finden sind, einem der besten Plätze der Welt. „Ich habe nur elf Löcher gebaut", sagt der Designer Pete Dye über sein Meisterwerk direkt am Meer, „die anderen sieben hat der liebe Gott gemacht." Bei so viel Weltklasse-Golf wird das Resort in der Dominikanischen Republik mit seinem eleganten, geradlinigen Interieur fast zur Nebensache. Das gute Leben spielt sich draußen ab. Casa de Campo ist berühmt für seine Reitsport-Angebote: In den Ställen warten dutzende Pferde begierig auf einen Ausritt, und auf drei Polo-Plätzen können sich auch Anfänger an diesem gleichermaßen uralten wie elitären Sport versuchen. Den ereignisreichen Tag lässt man am hoteleigenen Minitas Beach bei einer der legendären Piña Coladas ausklingen, serviert in einer frisch gepflückten Ananas.

Une île au trésor dans les Caraïbes avec 63 trous, parmi lesquels figurent les 18 appartenant au splendide Teeth of the Dog, l'un des meilleurs parcours au monde – « je n'ai conçu que onze trous », confesse le créateur Pete Dye à propos de son chef-d'œuvre donnant directement sur la mer, « les sept autres sont l'œuvre du bon Dieu ». Avec un golf de cette classe, ce complexe de la République dominicaine apparaît presque comme accessoire, malgré son intérieur élégant aux lignes droites. La douceur de vivre s'entend à l'extérieur. Casa de Campo est célèbre pour ses sports équestres : dans les écuries, des dizaines de chevaux trépignent d'envie de faire une sortie ou d'initier leurs cavaliers, même débutants, au polo sur l'un des trois terrains de ce sport aussi ancien qu'élitiste. Les clients peuvent conclure leur intense journée sur la plage privée de l'hôtel Minitas Beach en sirotant une fameuse Piña Colada servie dans un ananas fraîchement cueilli.

Casa de Campo

P.O. Box 140, La Romana
Dominican Republic
T +1 800 8773 643, reserva@ccampo.com.do
www.casadecampo.com
Rooms: 215 rooms and villas.
Facilities: pool, golf, spa, tennis, restaurant, free parking.
Services: 24 h front desk, weddings, family program.
Located: 8 minutes from Casa de Campo/La Romana International Airport.

Casa de Campo Golf Courses

63 holes
Handicap: not specific
Design: Pete Dye and Alice Dye

Teeth of the Dog: style: jungle parkland and rock-toothed cove, 1971
The Links: style: inland links, 1974
Dye Fore: style: parkland across seaside cliffs, 2005

Sanctuary Cap Cana

Cap Cana, Dominican Republic

This posh resort in the Dominican Republic has big plans: Cap Cana wants to become the Monte Carlo of the Caribbean. Located just a few minutes from the international airport of Punta Cana, its beach is as white as the sand bunkers on the fabulous Punta Espada golf course, designed by champion Jack Nicklaus; two further Nicklaus courses are in the works. Punta Espada is already considered a classic: On hole 13, a par 3, there's nothing but deep-blue ocean between the tee and the flag. For those who prefer to enjoy water without the sand, the large resort boasts a selection of five different pools. A further highlight is the spa treatments, which, if desired, can even be enjoyed right at the lagoon. Even the wine cellar is unique with thousands of fine bottles from France, Italy, and the United States.

Das Nobelresort in der Dominikanischen Republik hat große Pläne: Cap Cana will das Monte Carlo der Karibik werden. Es ist nur wenige Minuten vom internationalen Flughafen Punta Cana entfernt und sein Strand glänzt ebenso weiß wie der Bunkersand des fabelhaften Golfplatzes Punta Espada, entworfen von Altmeister Jack Nicklaus – und zwei weitere Nicklaus-Plätze sind im Bau. Punta Espada gilt schon jetzt als Klassiker: An Bahn 13, einem Par 3, ist zwischen Abschlag und Fahne nichts als tiefblauer Ozean. Wer das Wasser ohne Sand genießen mag, hat im großen Resort Sanctuary fünf Pools zur Auswahl. Eine Besonderheit sind die Spa-Behandlungen, die man auf Wunsch direkt an der Lagune genießen kann. Auch der Weinkeller mit tausenden edelster Flaschen aus Frankreich, Italien und den USA ist einmalig.

Ce complexe luxueux de la République dominicaine ne manque pas d'ambition : Cap Cana veut devenir le Monte-Carlo des Caraïbes. Quelques minutes à peine séparent Punta Cana de l'aéroport international. Sa plage rivalise de blancheur éclatante avec le sable des bunkers de fabuleux parcours Punta Espada, signés par l'ancien champion Jack Nicklaus – deux autres parcours de sa griffe sont même en construction. Punta Espada fait déjà figure de classique : le départ du numéro 13, un par 3, n'est séparé du drapeau que par l'azur profond de l'océan. Pour les baigneurs allergiques au sable, le grand complexe Sanctuary propose cinq piscines. Selon le désir du client, le spa propose également ses soins directement au bord de la lagune. Tout aussi unique, la cave à vin compte des milliers de bouteilles exceptionnelles venant de France, d'Italie et des États-Unis.

Sanctuary Cap Cana

22000 Cap Cana
Dominican Republic
T +1 866 8554 886
www.grandresortsatcapcana.com
Rooms: 176 suites and villas.
Facilities: spa, golf, beach, pools, tennis, bars, restaurants.
Services: Free parking, 24 h concierge and room service.
Located: 15 minutes from Punta Cana International Airport.

Punta Espada Golf Course

18 holes, 7,396 yards, par 72
Handicap: not specific
Style: parkland along Caribbean's coastline
Design: Jack Nicklaus, 2006

Banyan Tree Phuket

Phuket, Thailand

On the northwest coast of the island of Phuket, this resort on Bang Tao Bay does not flaunt its luxuriousness; instead, it prefers to celebrate it quietly. Small, freestanding villas with small pagoda roofs are tucked into the tropical vegetation. The resort's Laguna Phuket Golf Club offers a somewhat shorter course, but it will soon receive a 382-yard addition. Hole 12 is unique with a sharp dogleg to the right: The green is completely defended by a curving bunker. At the spa, the Royal Banyan treatment promises three hours of pure indulgence and features East-meets-West massage techniques. Guests who would like to experience something extraordinary should look into elephant trekking. The hour-long trek on an elephant, guided by an experienced mahout (elephant trainer), takes riders through the jungle and across smaller streams. There's no need to worry—perched on top of their elephant at 13 feet above ground, guests will stay high and dry.

An der Nordwestküste der Insel Phuket kehrt dieses Resort an der Bang Tao Bay seinen Luxus nicht opulent nach außen, sondern überzeugt eher im Stillen. Kleine, freistehende Villen mit Pagodendächern verstecken sich hinter tropischer Vegetation. Der zum Resort gehörende Laguna Phuket Golf Club bietet einen eher kurzen Course, soll aber demnächst um gut 350 Meter verlängert werden. Eine Besonderheit ist Bahn 12, ein scharfes Dogleg nach rechts: Das Grün ist komplett von einem kreisförmigen Bunker verteidigt. Im Spa verheißt die „Royal Banyan"-Behandlung eine dreistündige Verwöhn-Zeremonie mit östlichen und westlichen Massage-techniken. Wer etwas Außergewöhnliches erleben will, sollte den Ausritt auf einem Elefanten buchen. Die Tour führt eine Stunde lang mit einem „mahut", einem erfahrenen Elefantenführer, quer durch den Dschungel und kleinere Flüsse. Keine Sorge: Der Gast wird in vier Metern Höhe natürlich nicht nass.

Sur la côte nord-ouest de l'île de Phuket, ce complexe de la baie de Bang Tao n'affiche pas un luxe débordant ou ostentatoire : tout est dans le style. En effet, de petites villas indépendantes aux toits de pagode se fondent dans la végétation tropicale. Le complexe, avec son Laguna Phuket Golf Club, offre un parcours certes relativement court, mais qui sera prochainement rallongé de 350 mètres. Le numéro 12 est un dog-leg particulièrement difficile et tournant à droite : le green est complètement cerné par un bunker. Dans le spa, le programme « Royal Banyan » est une cérémonie de trois heures de soins mariant techniques orientales et occidentales. Les personnes à la recherche d'exotisme essaieront une balade à dos d'éléphant. Votre « mahut », ou cornac, vous guidera pendant une heure à travers la jungle et les zones d'eau. Mais soyez sans crainte, le passager est installé à quatre mètres de hauteur et ne risque pas de se mouiller.

Banyan Tree Phuket

33, 33/27 Moo 4, Srisoonthorn Road, 83110 Phuket
Thailand
T +66 763 243 74, phuket@banyantree.com
www.banyantree.com/en/phuket
Rooms: 132 rooms, suites, and villas.
Facilities: 5 restaurants, 2 bars, library, gym, golf, tennis, pools, spa, beach, scuba diving, sailing, canoeing, windsurfing,
classes in meditation, yoga, tai chi, aerobics, cooking classes.
Services: 24 h front desk, babysitting, free parking, WiFi.
Located: 20 minutes from Phuket International Airport.

Laguna Phuket Golf Club

34 Moo 4, Srisoonthorn Road, Cherngtalay Thalang, Phuket 83110
Thailand
T +66 762 709 91/2, golf@lagunaphuket.com
www.lagunaphuketgolf.com

Laguna Phuket Golf Course

18 holes, 6,654 yards, par 71
Handicap: not specific
Style: tropical scenic parkland with backdrop of
mountains and nearby sea
Design: Max Wexler and David Abell, 1990

Kirimaya

Khao Yai, Thailand

Thailand has recently become an outstanding golf destination. Kirimaya resort, about 62 miles northeast of Bangkok, borders Khao Yai National Park. The resort may offer just one of the over 150 golf courses in the country—but what a course! Designed by Jack Nicklaus, the course captivates with its lush vegetation, numerous bunkers, and water hazards, but contrasts them with flatter fairways and generous greens. Guests can take guided tours of the national park, where they can observe elephants, water buffalo, and gibbons. With a bit of luck, they might even snap a picture of Asiatic black bears, leopards, and even a rare tiger. It's not just Kirimaya's remote paradise location that promises relaxation. The spa offers massages with red wine extract among other treatments. Those who prefer to drink their wine can stop by Acala Restaurant and take in the sunset while enjoying a glass of one of many international vintages.

Thailand ist in den letzten Jahren zu einem herausragenden Golfziel geworden. Das Kirimaya-Resort 100 Kilometer nordöstlich von Bangkok liegt direkt am Khao-Yai-Nationalpark und bietet nur einen von mehr als 150 Plätzen des Landes – aber was für einen: Das Jack-Nicklaus-Design in prächtiger Vegetation besticht durch Unmengen von Bunkern und Wasserhindernissen; dafür sind die Fairways eher flach, die Grüns großzügig. Im Nationalpark lassen sich auf geführten Touren Elefanten, Wasserbüffel und Gibbon-Affen beobachten. Mit etwas Glück geraten auch Kragenbären, Leoparden und sogar die seltenen Tiger vor die Kamera. Doch Kirimaya verspricht nicht nur durch seine Lage in paradiesischer Abgeschiedenheit Entspannung. Das Spa offeriert unter anderem Massagen mit Rotwein-Extrakt. Wer den Wein eher im Körperinneren schätzt, kann im Restaurant Acala den Sonnenuntergang bei internationalen Spitzengewächsen genießen.

La Thaïlande s'est muée au cours des dernières années en une très importante destination de golf. Le complexe de Kirimaya situé à 100 kilomètres de Bangkok aux portes du parc national de Khao Yai n'offre certes qu'un des 150 golfs que compte le pays – mais quel golf ! La conception signée Jack Nicklaus fascine par la végétation abondante, mais surtout par la quantité de bunker et obstacles d'eau ; les fairways sont en revanche sans dénivelé et les greens bien vastes. Les excursions guidées dans le parc national permettent d'observer des éléphants, des buffles d'Asie et des gibbons, et parfois, avec de la chance, des ours à collier, des léopards et même, malgré leur rareté, des tigres. Kirimaya garantit une détente absolue grâce à son cadre paradisiaque et isolé. De plus, le spa propose notamment des massages aux extraits de vin rouge. Pour ceux qui doutent de l'application cutanée du vin, le restaurant Acala propose également de nombreux crus internationaux à savourer devant un coucher du soleil.

Kirimaya

1/3 Moo 6 Thanarat Road, Moo-Si, Khao Yai
Thailand
T +66 444 260 00, reservation@kirimaya.com
www.kirimaya.com/resort
Rooms: 56 rooms and suites, 64 villas.
Facilities: 2 restaurants, 1 bar, spa, gym, golf, pool.
Services: airport transfer upon request, shuttle to local village.
Located: at Khao Yai National Park, 2 hours from Bangkok.

Kirimaya Golf Course

18 holes, 7,115 yards, par 72
Handicap: not specific
Style: natural parkland
Design: Jack Nicklaus, 2004

Mandarin Oriental Dhara Dhevi

Chiang Mai, Thailand

This resort in Northern Thailand sets standards because it skillfully combines exuberant luxury with regional traditions and styles. The fairytale Lanna architecture of Chiang Mai is brilliantly reflected in the hotel's structures, which in turn are harmoniously integrated into the landscape. Three 18-hole golf courses near the resort will keep even the most demanding golfers entertained. The Green Valley Country Club is not only long but also replete with bunkers and water hazards. The undulating greens are particularly challenging at the Royal Chiang Mai Golf Resort, while at the fairly new Chiang Mai Highlands Golf Club, the best is saved for last at hole 18, a formidable par 5. Back at the hotel spa, the Royal Thai Ceremony is three and a half hours of pure indulgence. After so much R&R, those who don't want to miss out on city life should dive into the hubbub of Chiang Mai's famous night bazaar.

Das Resort im Norden Thailands setzt Maßstäbe, weil es den überbordenden Luxus gekonnt mit heimischen Traditionen und Stilen kombiniert. So spiegelt sich die märchenhafte Lanna-Architektur Chiang Mais brillant in den Hotelbauten, die ihrerseits harmonisch in die Landschaft eingebettet sind. Drei 18-Loch-Plätze in der Nähe des Resorts lassen selbst bei verwöhnten Golfern keine Langeweile aufkommen; der Green Valley Country Club ist nicht nur lang, sondern auch wasser- und bunkerreich. Im Royal Chiang Mai Golf Resort sorgen vor allem die welligen Grüns für Schwierigkeiten, während im recht neuen Chiang Mai Highlands Golf Club mit der 18, einem gewaltigen Par 5, das Beste zum Schluss kommt. Zurück im Hotel-Spa wartet mit der „Royal Thai Ceremony" ein dreieinhalbstündiges Verwöhn-programm. Wer nach so viel Entschleunigung auf das Stadtleben nicht verzichten will, sollte sich in den Trubel von Chiang Mais legendärem Nachtbasar stürzen.

Le complexe du nord de la Thaïlande établit une nouvelle référence, car il réussit le tour de force d'associer un luxe foisonnant aux traditions et aux styles locaux. En effet, la merveilleuse architecture Lanna de Chiang Mai se reflète avec brio dans les constructions de l'hôtel qui s'intègrent harmonieusement dans le paysage. Trois 18-trous proches du complexe satisferont même les golfeurs les plus exigeants. Le Green Valley Country Club est particulièrement long et présente de nombreux bunkers et obstacles d'eau ; le Royal Chiang Mai Golf Resort concentre ses difficultés surtout dans les greens ondulés, alors que le tout nouveau Chiang Mai Highlands Golf Club réserve le meilleur pour la fin, le 18, avec un puissant par 5. De retour à l'hôtel, le spa dorlote les clients avec un programme de soin de trois heures et demie intitulé « Royal Thai Ceremony ». Après un tel relâchement, ceux qui veulent retrouver les tumultes de la ville doivent se plonger dans l'animation du légendaire bazar nocturne de Chiang Mai.

Mandarin Oriental Dhara Dhevi

51/4 Chiang Mai - Sankampaeng Road Moo 1 T. Tasala A. Muang, 50000 Chiang Mai
Thailand
T +66 538 889 29, mocnx-reservations@mohg.com
www.mandarinoriental.com/chiangmai
Rooms: 123 rooms and suites.
Facilities: 9 restaurants and bars, library, spa, pools, gym, garden, parking lot, disabled facilities.
Services: car rental, valet parking, babysitting, airport transfer.
Located: 7.5 miles (12 kilometers) from Chiang Mai International Airport.

Chiang Mai Green Valley Country Club

Mae Sa, Mae Rim, Chiang Mai
Thailand
T +66 532 982 22
18 holes, 7,177 yards, par 72
Handicap: not specific
Style: palm tree-lined parkland
Design: Denis Griffiths & Associates, 1990

The Royal Chiang Mai Golf Resort

169 Moo 5, Chiang Mai-Prao Road Km 26, T.Maefak, A.Sansai,
Chiang Mai
Thailand
T +66 538 493 01, golf1@royalchiangmai.com
www.royalchiangmai.com
18 holes, 6,969 yards, par 72
Handicap: not specific
Style: hilly parkland
Design: Peter Thomas, 1996

Chiang Mai Highland Golf Club

167 Moo 2, Onuar, Mae On, Chiang Mai
Thailand
www.chiangmaihighlands.com/golf.html
18 holes, 7,049 yards, par 72
Handicap: not specific
Style: mountainside links
Design: Lee Schmidt of Schmidt-Curley Designer Company, 2006

The Club Saujana Resort Kuala Lumpur

Shah Alam, Malaysia

Just a half hour outside of Kuala Lumpur and yet a completely different world: Here, travelers can enjoy luxurious seclusion amid tropical gardens surrounded by two 18-hole courses, designed by Ronald Fream. The Palm course is often called "the cobra" due to its terrifying layout: Hole 2 is considered one of the most difficult short holes in Asia. Bunga Raya has the equally unsettling nickname "the crocodile." With its open fairways, the crocodile is often considered the slightly easier course, yet players would be wise not to underestimate it due to its numerous water hazards. Guests who would like to sample the spicy fare of their host country should treat themselves to specialties offered by the neighboring hotel's restaurant Sri Melaka—an exciting mixture of typically Malaysian, Chinese, and Portuguese flavors.

Nur eine halbe Stunde entfernt von der Metropole Kuala Lumpur und doch in einer ganz anderen Welt: Inmitten tropischer Gärten und umgeben von zwei 18-Loch-Plätzen genießt der Reisende luxuriöse Abgeschiedenheit. Die Plätze wurden von Ronald Fream entworfen. Der Palm Course trägt wegen seines furchteinflößenden Layouts den Spitznamen „Kobra"; bereits Bahn 2 gilt als eines der schwierigsten kurzen Löcher Asiens. Der Bunga Raya Course hat den kaum weniger beunruhigenden Beinamen „Krokodil". Das Krokodil gilt mit seinen offenen Fairways als etwas leichterer Platz, darf aber wegen der vielen Wasserhindernisse nicht unterschätzt werden. Wer die würzigen Noten des Gastgeberlands erschmecken will, sollte sich die Spezialitäten im benachbarten Hotelrestaurant Sri Melaka gönnen: eine spannende Mixtur aus typisch malaysischen, chinesischen und portugiesischen Aromen.

Situé à une demi-heure à peine de Kuala Lumpur, c'est pourtant un tout autre monde qui s'offre : au milieu de jardins tropicaux et de deux golfs 18-trous, les visiteurs découvrent les plaisirs d'une retraite luxueuse. Des deux terrains conçus par Ronald Fream, le Palm, surnommé « le Cobra », est le plus intimidant ; le numéro 2, par exemple, est connu pour être l'un des trous de courte distance les plus difficiles d'Asie. Le parcours Bunga Raya, dit « le Crocodile », n'est pas moins inquiétant ; bien qu'il soit réputé légèrement plus facile en raison de ses vastes fairways, il ne faut en aucun cas sous-estimer ses nombreux obstacles d'eau. Pour découvrir les saveurs épicées du pays, il faut déguster les spécialités du Sri Melaka, le restaurant de l'hôtel voisin qui propose une intéressante association d'arômes malaisiens, chinois et portugais.

The Club Saujana Resort Kuala Lumpur

Jalan Lapangan Terbang SAAS, 40150 Kuala Lumpur
Malaysia
T +60 378 431 234 , info@thesaujana.com
www.theclubatthesaujana-kl.com/ppc
Rooms: 27 rooms and 78 suites.
Facilities: restaurant, lounge, boutique, spa, pool, tennis, squash, sauna.
Services: 24 h concierge and room service, sightseeing tours, limousine service, personal shopping service.
Located: 30 minutes from Kuala Lumpur city center and 35 minutes from Kuala Lumpur International Airport.

Saujana Golf and Country Club

Saujana Resort Seksyen U2, 40150 Shah Alam, Selangor
Malaysia
T +60 378 461 466, golf@saujana.com.my
www.saujana.com.my

Palm Course

18 holes, 6,992 yards, par 72
Handicap: male 24, female 36
Style: jungle
Design: Ronald Fream, 1986

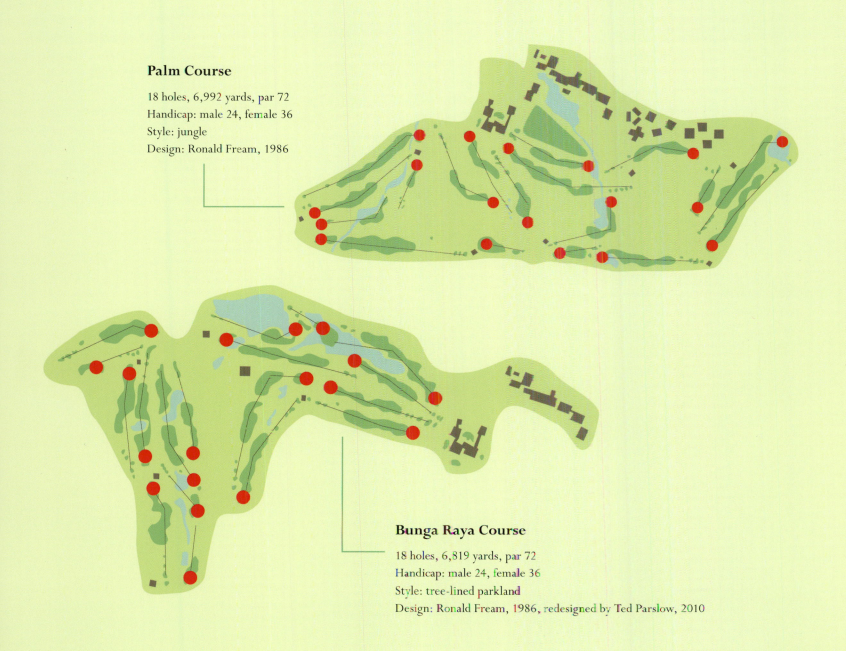

Bunga Raya Course

18 holes, 6,819 yards, par 72
Handicap: male 24, female 36
Style: tree-lined parkland
Design: Ronald Fream, 1986, redesigned by Ted Parslow, 2010

Mission Hills Haikou

Haikou, China

Hainan is an island in the South China Sea where Brian Curley was able to give free rein to his creativity. In a popular vacation area near Haikou, the island's capital, the golf course architect designed ten courses, almost single-handedly creating the second-largest golf resort in the world (the Mission Hills Resort Shenzhen near Hong Kong offers just two courses more). In addition, Hank Haney, Tiger Woods' former coach, has opened a branch of his golf school here. Golf lovers will be in utter bliss in the opulence they find at this resort. Visitors may find themselves reborn in the spa where some treatments can last half a day. To bring the day to a perfect close, guests can choose from twelve restaurants. The bright rooms and suites of Mission Hills Resort Haikou are decorated in light, natural tones, and Asian-inspired accents give the modern design its individuality.

Hainan ist eine Insel im Südchinesischen Meer, auf der sich Brian Curley austoben durfte. Gleich zehn Plätze erschuf der Designer in der beliebten Urlaubsregion nahe der Insel-Hauptstadt Haikou – und baute damit nahezu im Alleingang das zweitgrößte Golfresort der Welt (nur das Mission Hills Resort Shenzhen bei Hongkong bietet noch zwei Plätze mehr). Dazu unterhält Hank Haney, der ehemalige Coach von Tiger Woods, eine Dependance seiner Golfschule. Wer den Sport liebt, findet in dieser Üppigkeit das vollkommene Glück. Ein neuer Mensch darf man im Spa werden, in dem Behandlungen auch mal einen halben Tag dauern können; für den Schlussakkord des Tages stehen zwölf Restaurants zur Verfügung. Die lichtdurchfluteten Zimmer und Suiten des Mission Hills Resorts Haikou sind in hellen Naturtönen gehalten, asiatisch inspirierte Akzente verleihen dem modernen Design seine Individualität.

Il existe en mer de Chine méridionale une île où Brian Curley a pu montrer toute l'étendue de son talent : Hainan. En effet, l'architecte a conçu, près de Haikou, la très courue capitale de l'île, pas moins de dix terrains, créant ainsi le second complexe de golf au monde par la taille (après le Mission Hills Resort Shenzhen près de Hong Kong qui compte douze parcours). Tout amoureux de ce sport trouvera certainement dans cette abondance le bonheur absolu, d'autant plus que Hank Haney, l'ancien entraîneur de Tiger Woods, y a installé une filiale de son école de golf. Le spa s'occupera de régénérer les corps épuisés grâce à des soins pouvant durer une demi-journée entière. L'un des douze restaurants que compte l'établissement apportera la touche finale de la journée. Les chambres et suites baignées de lumière sont décorées dans des tons clairs et naturels. Le design moderne du complexe se teinte de notes asiatiques pour lui conférer toute son identité.

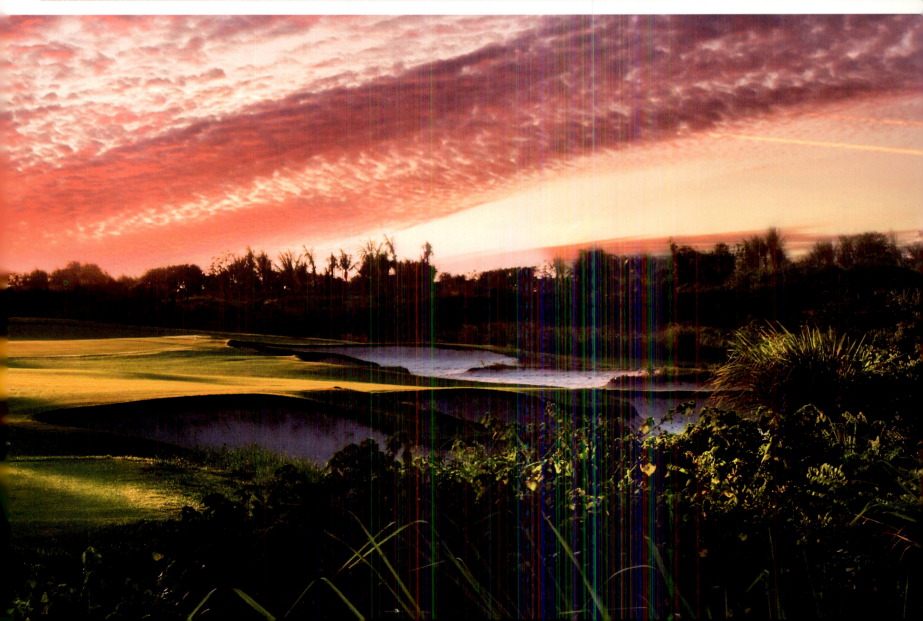

Mission Hills Haikou

No.1 Mission Hills Boulevard, 571155 Haikou, Hainan
China
T +86 898 686 838 88, info@missionhillschina.com
www.missionhillschina.com
Rooms: 518 rooms and suites.
Facilities: clubhouse, Hank Haney Golf Academy, meeting facilities, 12 restaurants, sports and recreation center, aquatic theme park, therapeutic volcanic mineral springs, spa oasis, shopping arcade.
Services: 24 h front desk, concierge service, laundry.
Located: 15 minutes from Haikou Meilan International Airport.

Meadow Links Course

18 holes, 6,673 yards, par 70
Handicap: male 24, female 36
Style: traditional East Coast golf course
Design: Brian Curley, 2011

Stone Quarry Course

18 holes, 6,029 yards, par 70
Handicap: male 24, female 36
Style: Pete Dye inspired design with wild-ride features
Design: Brian Curley, 2010

Blackstone Course

18 holes, 7,808 yards, par 73
Handicap: male 24, female 36
Style: natural layout with irregular bunker edges
Design: Brian Curley, 2010

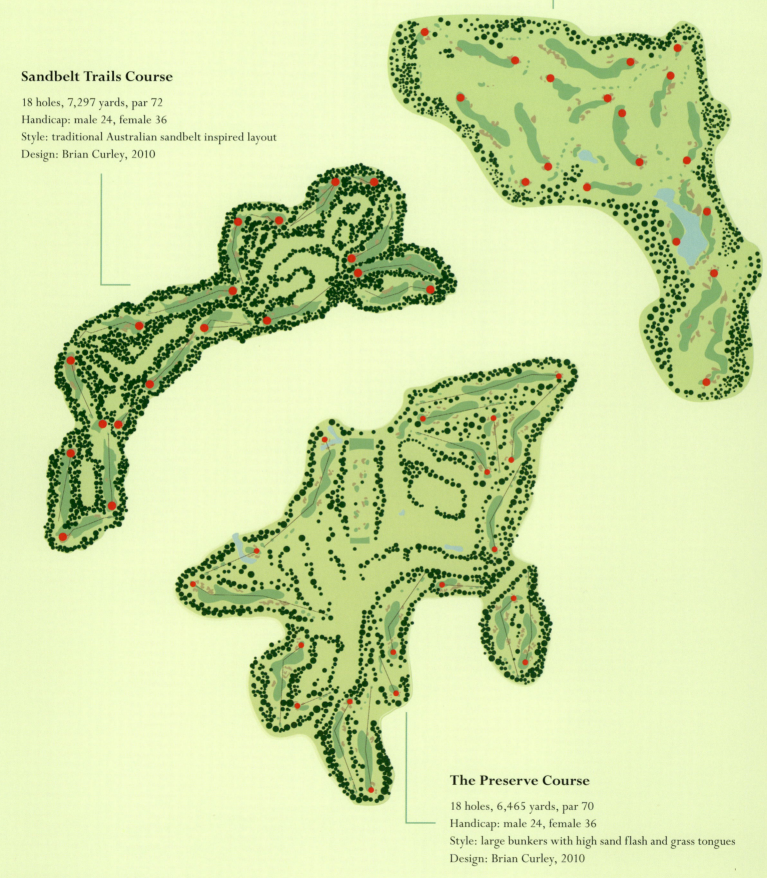

Lava Field Course

18 holes, 7,475 yards, par 72
Handicap: male 24, female 36
Style: natural, rugged golf course similar to The Blackstone Course
Design: Brian Curley, 2010

Sandbelt Trails Course

18 holes, 7,297 yards, par 72
Handicap: male 24, female 36
Style: traditional Australian sandbelt inspired layout
Design: Brian Curley, 2010

The Preserve Course

18 holes, 6,465 yards, par 70
Handicap: male 24, female 36
Style: large bunkers with high sand flash and grass tongues
Design: Brian Curley, 2010

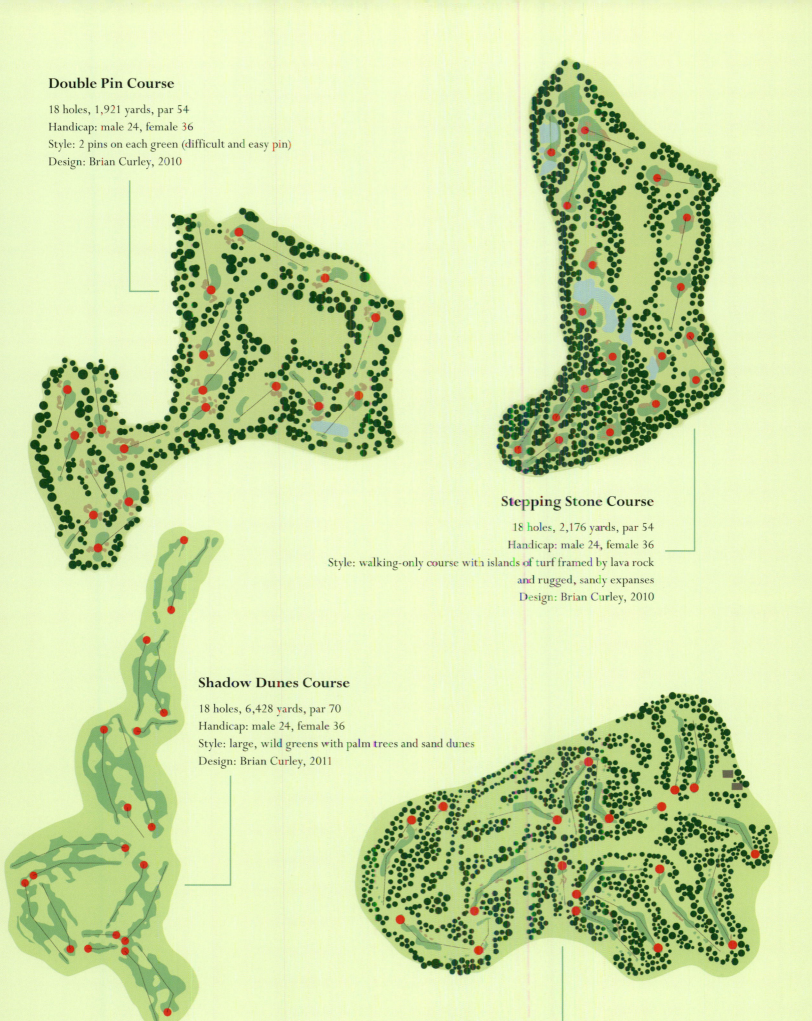

Double Pin Course

18 holes, 1,921 yards, par 54
Handicap: male 24, female 36
Style: 2 pins on each green (difficult and easy pin)
Design: Brian Curley, 2010

Stepping Stone Course

18 holes, 2,176 yards, par 54
Handicap: male 24, female 36
Style: walking-only course with islands of turf framed by lava rock
and rugged, sandy expanses
Design: Brian Curley, 2010

Shadow Dunes Course

18 holes, 6,428 yards, par 70
Handicap: male 24, female 36
Style: large, wild greens with palm trees and sand dunes
Design: Brian Curley, 2011

The Vintage Course

18 holes, 7,363 yards, par 72
Handicap: male 24, female 36
Style: traditional "lay of the land" golden age golf course
Design: Brian Curley, 2010

Amanusa

Bali, Indonesia

Grand luxury on a very small scale: With just 35 suites—all of which are individual villas, some with a private pool and a view of the Indian Ocean—unlimited privacy is guaranteed on Bali's southern peninsula. The Beach Club offers private beach cabins, beverages, and snacks. Early risers can enjoy breakfast on the beach while watching the sun rise, and night owls might prefer the barbeque by candlelight. Guests can enjoy snorkeling and exploring the colorful underwater world of the nearby coral reef, while a catamaran stands at the ready for longer trips. Both highly diverse and perfectly maintained, the Bali Golf & Country Club between the hotel and the beach leaves nothing to be desired. Some of the bunkers are quite deep and reminiscent of the links courses in Scotland. None other than Sir Nick Faldo holds the course record: The six-time Majors Champion finished the par 72 layout in just 63 strokes.

Großer Luxus im Kleinstformat: Nur 35 Suiten – auf einzeln stehende Villen aufgeteilt und zum Teil mit eigenem Pool und Blick auf den Indischen Ozean ausgestattet – garantieren grenzenlose Intimität auf Balis südlicher Halbinsel. Am Beach Club warten private Strandkabinen, Getränke und Snacks. Für Frühaufsteher wird die erste Mahlzeit des Tages zum Sonnenaufgang am Strand serviert, Nachtaktive genießen hier lieber das Barbecue bei Kerzenlicht. Die bunte Unterwasserwelt des nahen Korallenriffs kann erschnorchelt werden, während für längere Touren ein Katamaran bereitsteht. Der Bali Golf & Country Club zwischen Hotel und Strand lässt keine Wünsche offen, denn er ist abwechslungsreich und perfekt gepflegt. Die teilweise tiefen Bunker erinnern an schottische Links-Plätze. Den Platzrekord hält kein Geringerer als Sir Nick Faldo: Der sechsfache Major-Champion absolvierte das Par-72-Layout in 63 Schlägen.

Le grand luxe dans le plus petit des formats : le nombre limité de 35 suites – réparties dans plusieurs villas indépendantes, dont certaines avec piscine privée et vue sur l'océan Indien – garantit une intimité absolue sur la presqu'île sud de Bali. Le club de plage dispose de cabines et d'un bar proposant boissons et amuse-bouches. Les lève-tôt apprécieront le petit-déjeuner servi dès le lever du jour sur la plage, tandis que les noctambules préféreront les barbecues à la lumière des flambeaux. Le monde sous-marin et multicolore de la barrière de corail toute proche peut être exploré avec masque et tuba. Pour les sorties plus longues, un catamaran est à disposition. Le Bali Golf & Country Club situé entre l'hôtel et la plage comblera les joueurs par la qualité de l'entretien et la diversité du parcours. Les bunkers parfois profonds rappellent les links écossais. Le record du parcours par-72 a été réalisé en 63 coups par, excusez du peu, le sextuple vainqueur de titres majeurs Sir Nick Faldo.

Amanusa

Jalan Pantai Mengiat, 80363 Nusa Dua, Bali
Indonesia
T +62 361 772 333, amanusa@amanresorts.com
www.amanusa.com
Rooms: 35 suites.
Facilities: 3 restaurants, 1 bar, spa, pool, beach club, tennis, golf, library, boutique.
Services: 24 h private dining.
Located: 20 minutes from Bali Airport (Ngurah Rai) Denpasar.

The Bali Golf and Country Club

Kawasan Wisata, Nusa Dua, 80363 Bali
Indonesia
T +62 361 771 791, marketing@baligolfandcountryclub.com
www.baligolfandcountryclub.com

The Bali Golf and Country Club Course

18 holes, 6,888 yards, par 72
Handicap: 36
Style: seaside parkland
Design: Robin Nelson and Rodney Wright, 1991

Hyatt Regency Coolum, Golf Resort and Spa
Queensland, Australia

The Sunshine Coast lives up to its name: In the subtropical climate of Queensland, the sun shines almost year round. Set along an exquisite private beach at the base of Mount Coolum, this hotel allows guests to indulge in Australia's relaxing beach life, whether they choose to surf, snorkel, or kiteboard. Those who prefer a birds-eye view can climb Mount Coolum, an extinct volcano whose altitude of 680 feet shouldn't seriously frighten any climbers. The hotel's rooms and suites are located in many smaller buildings which are tucked into the lush, naturalistic grounds of the resort. Designed by Robert Trent Jones Jr., the golf course here is known for one thing in particular: numerous water hazards in the middle of the bush. The left side of the very first hole is completely wet, and players will find holes 9 to 15 quite challenging as well since they appear to have more water hazards than land.

Der Name Sunshine Coast lügt nicht: Die Sonne ist im subtropischen Klima von Queensland praktisch ganzjährig präsent. Am Fuß des Mount Coolum und direkt am feinen privaten Sandstrand können sich Gäste dem beneidenswert entspannten australischen Beach-Life hingeben, ob beim Surfen, Schnorcheln oder Kiten. Wer lieber den Blick von ganz oben genießt, der kann den Mount Coolum bezwingen, einen erloschenen Vulkan. Seine Höhe von 208 Metern dürfte keinen Kletterer ernsthaft schrecken. Die Zimmer und Suiten des Hotels sind geschickt auf viele kleinere Gebäude im natürlich gehaltenen und üppig bewachsenen Areal verteilt. Der Golfplatz von Robert Trent Jones Junior bietet vor allem eines: viele Wasserhindernisse inmitten des Buschlandes. Schon Bahn 1 ist auf der linken Seite komplett nass, und auf den Löchern 9 bis 15 scheint es mehr Seen als Landezonen zu geben.

Le nom de Sunshine Coast n'est pas le fruit du hasard : sous le climat subtropical du Queensland, le soleil brille pratiquement toute l'année. Les clients de l'hôtel peuvent dès lors se prélasser sur la plage de sable fin ou se saisir d'un surf, d'un cerf volant ou d'un masque et d'un tuba pour vivre l'Australian way of life au pied du mont Coolum. Ceux qui aiment les panoramas ne manqueront pas l'ascension de ce volcan éteint. Haut de 208 mètres, il ne devrait faire peur à aucun randonneur. Les chambres et les suites de l'hôtel sont judicieusement réparties dans plusieurs bâtiments sur un terrain à la végétation luxuriante et aménagé de manière naturelle. Le terrain de golf signé Robert Trent Jones Junior peut être résumé ainsi : de nombreux obstacles d'eau en plein cœur du bush. Le trou numéro 1 présente de l'eau sur tout son côté gauche et les trous 9 à 15 semblent compter plus de lacs que de terrain.

Hyatt Regency Coolum, Golf Resort and Spa

Warran Road, Coolum Beach 4573, Queensland
Australia
T +61 754 461 234, coolum.regency@hyatt.com
www.coolum.regency.hyatt.com
Rooms: 324 rooms, including studio suites and 2- and 3-bedroom villas.
Facilities: 5 restaurants, 3 bars, day spa, gym, beach club, tennis center, golf, business center, shops, boutique, art gallery, golf education center.
Services: 24 h front desk and valet parking, e-concierge, Camp Hyatt childcare, bicycle rental, shuttle service within resort, daytime shuttle to Noosa.
Located: 6 miles (10 kilometers) from Sunshine Coast Airport, 62 miles (100 kilometers) from Brisbane Domestic & International Airport.

Hyatt Regency Coolum Golf Course

18 holes, 6,712 yards (6,137 meters), par 72
Handicap: not specific
Style: tree-lined and open parkland
Design: Robert Trent Jones, Jr., 1988, renovation 2009

The Farm at Cape Kidnappers

Te Awanga, New Zealand

The most beautiful golf course in the world? Probably: It's hard to imagine a course with a more dramatic setting—on the cliffs near the ocean, in the middle of untouched nature. The resort cleverly plays up the advantages of its remote location by offering puritanical luxury with a raw and more rustic architectural style and restrained exteriors—this elegant hotel in Hawke's Bay initially comes across more like a secluded farm. U.S. golf course architect Tom Doak has created his masterpiece here, 459 feet above sea level: The golf course is already making history. Deep bunkers, undulating greens, and a constant wind provide for a challenging round of golf—but why worry about the score when you can relish the incredible views of waves crashing at the foot of the cliffs? Named Pirate's Plank, hole 15 is magnificent: a long par 5 that calls for incredible accuracy—otherwise the ball will be swallowed up by the ocean forever.

Ist dies der schönste Platz der Welt? Wahrscheinlich: Kaum ein anderer Course liegt so unmittelbar über Klippen in Meeresnähe, inmitten unberührter Natur. Das dazugehörige Resort spielt die Stärken der abgeschiedenen Lage geschickt aus, indem es Luxus ganz puritanisch offeriert, mit Architektur im rauen „Jurassic"-Stil und zurückhaltendem Äußeren – das edle Hotel in der Hawke's Bay wirkt zunächst eher wie eine abgeschiedene Farm. US-Designer Tom Doak hat hier, 140 Meter über dem Meeresspiegel, sein Meisterstück erschaffen; der Platz schreibt schon jetzt Geschichte. Tiefe Bunker, ondulierte Grüns und der beständige Wind sorgen für eine schwierige Golfrunde – doch wer hat schon den Score im Sinn, wenn es fabelhafte Ausblicke auf die Wellen zu genießen gibt, die sich am Fuß der Klippen brechen? Grandios ist die 15 namens „Pirate's Plank", ein langes Par 5, das unerbittliche Genauigkeit erfordert – sonst versinkt der Ball für immer im Ozean.

S'agit-il du plus bel endroit sur Terre ? Tout le porte à croire : aucun autre parcours en pleine nature ne surplombe ainsi la mer du haut de vertigineuses falaises. Le complexe attenant exploite adroitement les points forts de cet isolement en offrant un luxe austère avec une architecture associant un style brut et un extérieur tout en retenue – l'élégant hôtel sur Hawke's Bay fait avant tout l'effet d'une ferme isolée. L'architecte de golf américain Tom Doak a créé ici son chef-d'œuvre, 140 mètres au-dessus du niveau de la mer ; le parcours est déjà entré dans l'histoire. De profonds bunkers, des greens ondulés et le vent incessant garantissent une session difficile. Comment peut-on penser au score avec une vue si extraordinaire sur les vagues qui se brisent au pied des falaises ? Le 15, appelé « Pirate's Plank » est grandiose. Ce long par 5 requiert une précision effroyable – au risque de voir sa balle disparaître pour toujours dans l'océan.

The Farm at Cape Kidnappers

446 Clifton Road, Te Awanga
New Zealand
T +64 687 519 00, info@capekidnappers.com
www.capekidnappers.com

Rooms: 22 suites and The Owner's Cottage with 4 bedrooms.
Facilities: spa, gym, indoor pool, golf, disabled access, fireplaces, parking lot, 2 restaurants, bar.
Services: 24 h front desk, room movies, currency exchange.
Located: 6 hours from Auckland, 4 hours from Wellington, 2.5 hours from Taupo.

Cape Kidnappers Golf Course

18 holes, 7,119 yards, par 71
Handicap: 36
Style: modern parkland along coastline
Design: Tom Doak, 2004

Kauri Cliffs

Matauri Bay, New Zealand

What a panorama! The Pacific, cliffs, and rocks as far as the eye can see—it's unlikely that any other hotel has more ocean views. The golf course is as spectacular as the hotel. Although many clubs boast about their ocean view, the Kauri Cliffs course leaves the competition in the dust: After a poor drive, players can console themselves with amazing ocean views from 15 holes. New Zealand golf superstar Michael Campbell is one of many fans of the spectacular layout. With its 22 suites, the lodge strikes a balance between modest colonial luxury and a modern interpretation of country style—which just goes to show that even small hotels can epitomize greatness. Three private beaches invite guests to rest and relax. A day oceanside comes to a satisfying close with a barbeque, exclusively prepared by the resort's chef de cuisine, while guests soak up the sunset and sip some of the best wines New Zealand has to offer.

Was für ein Panorama! Pazifik, Klippen und Felsen, so weit das Auge reicht – wohl nirgendwo sonst darf man mehr Meer genießen. Auch der Golfplatz steht nicht hinter dem Hotel zurück. Viele Clubs prahlen mit Meerblick, aber der Kauri Cliffs Golf Course lässt die Konkurrenz weit hinter sich: Auf gleich 15 Bahnen können sich die Spieler nach schlechten Schlägen mit Ozean-Sicht trösten. Nicht nur Neuseelands Golf-Superstar Michael Campbell ist ein Fan des spektakulären Layouts. Die Lodge mit ihren 22 Suiten verbreitet ein Ambiente zwischen dezentem kolonialem Luxus und modern interpretiertem Country-Stil und beweist: Auch kleine Hotels können viel Größe zeigen. Gleich drei private Strände laden zum süßen Nichtstun ein. Der Tag am Meer endet stimmungsvoll bei einem Barbecue, exklusiv zubereitet vom Küchenchef des Resorts, begleitet vom Sonnenuntergang und den besten Weinen Neuseelands.

Quelle vue ! Le Pacifique, les falaises et les récifs, aussi loin que porte le regard. Impossible de trouver meilleur endroit pour admirer la mer. De nombreux clubs se targuent d'avoir vue sur la mer, mais aucun ne peut rivaliser avec le Kauri Cliffs qui lui, n'a certainement pas relégué son parcours à l'arrière de l'hôtel : quinze trous avec vue sur l'océan – de quoi consoler ceux qui manqueraient leur coup. Le champion néo-zélandais Michael Campbell compte parmi les nombreux fidèles de ce spectaculaire terrain. Le lodge propose 22 suites dans une ambiance tout en retenue associant décor colonial luxueux et style campagnard revisité, ce qui prouve que les petits hôtels peuvent eux aussi afficher une certaine opulence. Trois plages privées invitent à la douce activité qu'est le farniente. Une journée de plage se termine par un barbecue convivial accompagné des meilleurs vins néo-zélandais avec le coucher de soleil en toile de fond.

Kauri Cliffs

Tepene Tabelands Road, 0245 Matauri Bay
New Zealand
T +64 940 700 10, info@kauricliffs.com
www.kauricliffs.com

Rooms: 22 suites and 1 cottage.
Facilities: dining indoor or on the verandas, hiking, golf, tennis, mountain biking, spa, indoor and outdoor pool, gym, private beaches, clay pigeon shooting.
Services: 24 h front desk, free parking, rooms for disabled.
Located: 25 minutes from Kerikeri Airport.

Kauri Cliffs Golf Course

18 holes, 7,119 yards, par 72
Handicap: 36
Style: seaside links style and open parkland
Design: David Harman of Golf Course Consultants, 2000

Photo Credits

Editor   Martin Nicholas Kunz
Texts   Stefan Maiwald
Copy Editing   Dr. Simone Bischoff, Janosch Müller, Jasmin Kriegelstein
Editorial Management   Miriam Bischoff
Art Direction   Martin Nicholas Kunz
Layout & Prepress   Sonja Oehmke
Photo Editing   David Burghardt, Julie Huehnken
Imaging   Tridix, Berlin
Translations by   Romina Russo, RR Communications
English   Heather Bock, Romina Russo
French   Thomas Vitasse, Pière Fuentes

Published by teNeues Publishing Group

teNeues Verlag GmbH + Co. KG
Am Selder 37, 47906 Kempen, Germany
Phone: +49 (0)2152 916 0, Fax: +49 (0)2152 916 111
e-mail: books@teneues.de

Press department: Andrea Rehn
Phone: +49 (0)2152 916 202
e-mail: arehn@teneues.de

teNeues Digital Media GmbH
Kohlfurter Straße 41-43, 10999 Berlin, Germany
Phone: +49 (0)30 700 77 65 0

teNeues Publishing Company
7 West 18th Street, New York, NY 10011, USA
Phone: +1 212 627 9090, Fax: +1 212 627 9511

teNeues Publishing UK Ltd.
21 Marlowe Court, Lymer Avenue, London SE19 1LP, UK
Phone: +44 (0)20 8670 7522, Fax: +44-(0)20 8670 7523

teNeues France S.A.R.L.
39, rue des Billets, 18250 Henrichemont, France
Phone: +33 (0)2 4826 9348, Fax: +33 (0)1 7072 3482

www.teneues.com

© 2012 teNeues Verlag GmbH + Co. KG, Kempen

ISBN: 978-3-8327-9614-3

Library of Congress Control Number: 2012932111

Printed in the Czech Republic.